A PLANT-BASED FARMHOUSE

A PLANT-BASED FARMHOUSE

Wholefood recipes from my house on the hill

CHERIE HAUSLER

murdoch books

Sydney | London

We acknowledge the traditional owners of the land on which this book was written and made: the Ngadjuri people, the Gadigal and Cammeraygal peoples of the Eora nation, the Wurundjeri people of the Kulin nation, the Wadawurrung people and the nipaluna people. We pay respect to the custodians of the lands on which the food that is within these pages was foraged, grown and sourced, and acknowledge the recipes and stories that have been shared on these lands for over 60,000 years.

contents

foreword

———

by Maggie Beer

Of all the people I know who have had a light step upon this earth, Cherie is one of the first who comes to mind. She emanates that perfect vision of health we all aspire to, and never seems to age, always living her best life.

Cherie's love of cooking and gardening is the core of her world. Oh, and her love of animals, too. Her celebration of plant-based foods, underpinned by the fruits and vegetables of the seasons, has been the very essence of the life she has built.

I first met Cherie more than 20 years ago on the set of a television show where she was co-presenter and I was a 'walk on'. I was out of my comfort zone, but immediately I was in awe of her presence and quick mind. And I then realised the bonus that we were both passionate Barossans!

I can't quite put my finger on when it was that we came to work together – it almost seems as though we always did. Cherie, truly multi-talented as a writer, designer, and stylist became part of our team in our early business, Maggie Beer Products. Whether it was helping me with gardening columns or press releases, or writing the 'romance' for my husband Colin's wine labels, Cherie put her hand skilfully to it all.

I'm thrilled she has channelled her combined talents into writing this beautiful book and sharing her table with you all. Her recipes are bursting with flavour and creativity, and are an important part of the food I love to eat. I hope you enjoy it as much as I do.

Maggie Beer

a common thread of food

———

Growing up in the Barossa Valley in South Australia,
I honestly thought I could outrun my small-town upbringing
when I left for bigger adventures — and I almost did, until I
needed to find common ground with a new work colleague
or flatmate, when the offer of a pot of tea or a homemade
cake seemed to speak the language of instant community
in a way I had completely underestimated.

My country childhood had educated me in what I would come to understand as the most potent language of all: good food and honest hospitality. Once I realised this, I stopped brushing off where I came from and started making a lot more cake.

After leaving the Barossa when I was 17 years old, in every big city I lived in around the world, whether it was Melbourne, Sydney, Bangkok or London, I would have unintentional 'country gatherings', where I would invite friends over and end up putting as many of my homegrown food memories on the table as possible. I'd set the table with any foliage I could find at the market that offered a seasonal nod to what I now forage for free along dirt roads; my instincts were always to recreate farmhouse living, despite being in a tiny city apartment. We grew our own food on our terrace rooftop, we had ducks to help out with the compost, and even now if I wander past our old studio apartment in Sydney's inner-city suburb of Surry Hills, I can see the legacy of vegies we grew in every available space along the back laneway.

While it wasn't necessarily obvious to me, when my mother-in-law told us about a 150-year-old stone farmhouse for sale on Koonunga Hill in the Barossa Valley, everyone could see the handwriting on the wall. We moved in just as the sheep were moving out. Well, almost. In renovating our new home, electricity was our first exciting achievement, closely followed by running water.

There's always a silver lining, though, and in our case, most of that came in edible form. We foraged for wild olives and learnt how to brine them. We turned windfall apples from a forgotten orchard into cider vinegar. We learnt how to bake sourdough, brew kombucha, blend tea. We set up a stall at the local farmers' market. We created community events at old railway stations, in the middle of vineyards, and among abandoned blacksmith shops and German-settler stone outbuildings. We were introduced to committees and horticultural societies, competed in the local agricultural show and ran workshops. Anywhere ladies were asked to bring a plate, I took one!

The biggest surprise was how easy it was to find familiar food territory with others, despite our plant-based eating habits.

I'm still amazed at the knowledge gained and conversations sparked from sharing something handmade and homegrown in a small community — tips on getting a good rise on your bread in winter (using an electric blanket), or which beans will hold their colour for pickling ('Lazy Housewife' runners), and where to find a secret patch of wild saffron (near the old footbridge on the River Light). The biggest surprise was how easy it was to find familiar food territory with others, despite our plant-based eating habits. As one lady said to me at a horticultural meeting, 'Oh, we all eat plants dear — nothing new in that.' Honest and to the point. And of course, she's right. So many traditional country foods and cooking methods have always been plant based, and with those that aren't, I haven't yet found any that can't be tweaked into a healthier version of themselves. No one need miss out, and I love that.

a plant-based journey

———

Lots of people ask what made me decide to shift from being vegetarian to completely plant-based. The first thing I'd emphasise is that it happened in increments. If you feel you're heading in that direction, it may not be one single incident that draws a line in the sand for you; for some people it's health, for some it's animal welfare, for some it's environmental concerns — and probably a host of other reasons.

At the age of 14, I boldly declared I was a vegetarian. My parents weren't surprised. From the age of two, I would squirrel away any meat dished up to me in the side of my cheek, saying I didn't like it, and never wanting to swallow it. Many years later, Dad joked he should have taken my plea as conviction rather than a childhood whim. 'You always had strong feelings about food,' he said. It's true, and it started early!

In the Barossa Valley, we lived in the middle of a vineyard Dad managed, and we also had a few sheep that were kept for meat. I was obsessed with the lambs, hoping at least one ewe would abandon her offspring each season so we'd have to bottle-feed it and keep it in a little yard next to the house. At a very young age, I also came to understand exactly where meat came from, because Dad would kill sheep or lambs for us to eat. It wasn't unusual in the country. Lots of families did the same, but it never made sense to me, and I never liked the taste or texture of meat. Most of the time, though, even while voicing my protests, I ate what was cooked for me. Until I could cook for myself.

When I announced my vegetarianism, Mum wasn't thrilled with the idea of cooking two

separate meals each night. 'That's okay,' I assured her, 'I can cook for myself.' Again with the bold statements. And so, with the only vegetarian books at our local library coming from America (can any of us even remember our lives pre-Google?), I set about looking for weird ingredients I'd never heard of and figuring out how many ounces were in a cup measure. It was the best crash course in cooking, and the first of many 'worthwhile hurdles' to jump. Mum often ate what I cooked, too, always showing lots of interest and encouragement, and letting me figure things out in my own way. I'm really grateful for that.

Understanding is ever evolving, and I've always tried to be open to new information along the way. In that manner of self-enquiry, I remember discovering that while cows need to give birth to calves every year to produce milk, goats can continue to produce milk for years after having a kid. I loved goat's cheese, and this seemed to be an improved approach to enjoying cheese, without needing to be part of the dairy story (for more on this, see the intro to the butter recipe on page 230) — so I took up the offer from one of our customers at the farmers' market to try milking her goat before deciding whether to keep one at our place.

I turned up to meet my friend's goat and the first thing that took me by surprise was that her nanny goat had a little kid. Watching as my friend separated the baby goat from her mother so I could milk her didn't quite fit the happy version of the story I had told myself before I arrived. My attention was brought back to the nanny goat when my friend started showing me how to milk

her. It was a slow, methodical process, and the nanny goat seemed completely at ease — until it was my turn. Again, I'm not sure why I was surprised, but I wasn't prepared for how warm the goat's udders would feel. It was a very real reminder that I was drawing milk from a living being. No machines, just my hands on her warm udders. I thought it would feel 'natural', but it felt uncomfortably intimate. It didn't help that I was like a fumbling teenager and the poor goat was having to endure my clunky lack of dexterity. As soon as I did finally manage to draw some milk from her, the baby goat started bleating. This wasn't what I'd hoped for! I continued, trying not to look at her little kid, trying not to hurt the goat, and all the while thinking that the only way this milk should be drawn from the goat's udder is by her baby's mouth, perfectly formed to fit around her mother's teat in order to be nourished with everything a baby goat needs — no risk of the milk spoiling because it's never exposed to the air, no need to store the milk because the kid can drink whenever hungry, no need to preserve the milk in the form of cheese because it is intended to be consumed immediately. Oh. Then the realisation. This is a system perfectly designed by Nature for a mother and her baby. Like any other mother and her baby. Why the heck would I force my way into this story? It was too sacred for me to claim any part to play. And so, I didn't. Not because I suddenly thought it was weird or wrong, but my first-hand experience had me so in awe of Nature's design, I deferred to that, and decided I wouldn't be getting a goat after all.

I didn't know that would be the day I wouldn't ever eat 'normal' cheese again — but as it turns out, it was. That's when I first started making cashew cheese.

joining the dots

———

If there was such a thing as a pendulum swing through food, I feel like I've covered a sizeable chunk of that journey — from homegrown, handmade recipes at one end of the arc, to the opposite extreme of commercial food created for national supermarket chains. Without any grand plan, the common thread of food has woven its way throughout almost every event, business and vegie garden planting I've ever done. And while I'd never suggest the entire timeline has been a walk in the park, I can't think of anything in my life that has been worthwhile doing as 'easy'. Maybe I'm wired to seek out challenge as giving purpose to what life throws our way.

At the pivotal age of 14, I had my first part-time job as a 'dishy' at one of the local restaurants attached to a winery just down the road. The chef was completely volatile at all times, but by offering only a positive attitude if he ever did deem to speak to me, I ended up learning so much from him. By the time I left that job, I knew how to make champagne ice cream, mix a decent salad dressing and grill a kangaroo steak. More good grounding for the future...

At 15 my girlfriend and I, both working in restaurants on the weekends, became obsessed with her mum's *Vogue Entertaining* magazines. Her mother threw the most amazing dinner

parties, and we were desperate to be adults, so we decided to start throwing amazing dinner parties too. We'd combine our 'worldly knowledge of cuisine', gleaned from washing dishes in country restaurants, with a well-curated menu straight from the pages of *Vogue*, and invited our 15-year-old friends, dressed accordingly, to the fanciest version of dinner we could imagine. Our parents were incredibly trusting, leaving the house to us while they went out to their own soirees. We'd plan the music, set the table, get dressed up and pretend we were sophisticated until the stroke of midnight turned us back into teenagers. It was so much fun, and that feeling of excitement in creating food experiences has never left me.

The world of restaurants was always familiar. Both of my parents worked in a restaurant at different stages, and if ever we went out for dinner, it was always a special occasion. I remember the potent mixture of aromas whenever I'd go into a restaurant as a kid — men's aftershave and grilled onions mixed with wine and women's perfume... never underestimate the power of aromatherapy when it comes to food memories. I blame this entirely for my eagerness to say yes when my brother suggested we set up a restaurant. In Bangkok. When neither of us had ever had a business before.

Eat Me opened 26 years ago during the global financial crisis of 1998. We managed to survive that, then there was a tsunami, and then the COVID pandemic came along — but somehow my brother steered the ship through all of it. I had the easy job of figuring out which tablecloths we'd have, or what vegetarian dishes we could put on the menu, or what the website would look like. Way back in the early days, I also worked in the kitchen, helping the guys out where I could, usually stationed in the cold kitchen making salads and desserts. I loved those days. When we couldn't get decent kalamata olives in Bangkok, I took them over in my suitcase from Sydney... along with olive oil, tea, sourdough starter, kombucha scobys — whatever it took to keep raising the bar and creating memorable food experiences at Eat Me. I can't tell you how many 'worthwhile hurdles' co-owning a restaurant has presented, but I also can't tell you how much I love walking up those stairs each time I visit. It's still my favourite restaurant.

It was Eat Me that led to my tea business Scullery Made, in a roundabout way. I was hand-blending teas for Eat Me so we could offer something no one else was doing in Bangkok, and when we moved back to the Barossa 20 years later and I started working with food legend Maggie Beer, I suggested she could do something similar at her Farm Shop, knowing how much she also valued special food experiences. I blended up some teas to show her what I was talking about, and next thing you know I have a tea business running out of the underground cellar in our farmhouse. It seemed right to refer to it as 'the scullery', and Scullery Made was born. I absolutely love tea and all that comes with the ritual of brewing proper tea in a tea pot, choosing a favourite cup, and taking a moment to breathe in that perfectly familiar smell, so those dots were not difficult to join at all.

Having Scullery Made led to 11 years' involvement with our local Barossa Farmers' Market, and because my interest in food was steadily shifting from vegetarian to vegan,

> The idea of bringing plant-based food made with recognisable ingredients into mainstream accessibility was too exciting to ignore, so our All The Things Food Range was launched.

I started making a small range of products that I couldn't get my hands on locally. Things like granola, butter, cashew cheese, kale chips, green smoothies, kombucha, and vegan cakes and tarts all became part of the offer across the trestle table each Saturday. There was always tea made from the thermos and groups of friends catching up — and these weekly morning gatherings led to community events and eventually a retail store in an old fire station.

Food styling and recipe writing were always in the mix, too, so when investors approached me to create a plant-based food range for supermarkets, I made the scary leap from handmade, small-batch recipes to HACCP-accredited commercial food production. The idea of bringing plant-based food made with recognisable ingredients (and no weird colours!) into mainstream accessibility was too exciting to ignore, and so our All The Things food range was launched in 2017. We developed so many products in the range, but it was our white mould cheeses that really took every bit of food experience I'd accumulated, and combined it with all the experience I didn't yet have, to pioneer something completely new in vegan cheese. We ended up in national supermarkets, as well as exporting, and while I will say that business put more hurdles in front of me than I could ever have imagined, once again it has led to where I am now.

I love that the brand had its own pendulum swing: from the stainless-steel enormity of our commercial kitchen back to small-scale events and workshops in my stable kitchen. We filmed two series of *All The Things* in that kitchen, and

I love how that familiarity puts everyone at ease when they first arrive for a workshop or gathering in the space now.

Without having the time to really notice the incremental change, the world of commercial food put to the test every skill I had gained over the years, but at the same time sapped me of the very thing that fired my creativity — time to grow food, cook food and eat well. Those dots have to be joined for me, or the beauty and balance of life goes out the window. That's when the pendulum started to swing back, and I've made it a priority to let lunches be long again. Cooking, sharing and eating food can be the best kind of life coach — clarifying what fuels us in all the important ways.

So much has been exchanged via the magical thread of growing and eating food, revisiting tried and tested ideas from the past, reclaiming and recycling concepts of building and gardening, cooking and foraging — and I hope that learning never stops. But for me, it's not just about rehashing old traditions for the sake of their history, it's about finding ways to apply those kernels of learning to the way I find myself living in the Barossa now: understanding distilling in order to extract our own essential oils, or knowing enough about fermentation to lead to our own version of cheesemaking — always looking for a way to honour traditional methods with non-traditional ingredients.

Life here isn't just about eating good food; it's about growing it, harvesting it, preserving it, reinventing it and sharing it.

I hope the following pages will be dog-eared and tea-stained in no time from regular use, but the real excitement for me would be to know that you find even the smallest inspiration in what I have shared — whether that's to grow a pot of herbs on a windowsill, or take a moment to smell that fresh peach before you bite into it, or to bring the daily ritual of tea drinking into your life without anything 'fast' or 'convenient' about it.

Anywhere you can add in some good stuff is a lovely thing, isn't it? Let's go with that plan; it's my kind of gratitude practice.

Now, what shall we cook first?

a few extra notes

———

There's a lot to convey in a cookbook, and while I don't want to overwhelm you with too much information, I also want to make sure I've shared the things I think make a big difference to the amount of time you spend in the kitchen, and how you feel when you're there.

I always start with the simplest premise: make things with your hands and eat them. But there's always more to learn and more to care about — and with more choices being presented to all of us all the time, the most basic approach to food can quickly become muddied with an overload of gadgets, opinions and further questions.

I'm hoping this book heads in the opposite direction to food overwhelm, and instead invites you to let your unique connection to food be at the centre of your cooking. Growing food is a fast-track to that connection for me, but I get that not all of us can — or want to — grow food. Maybe for you it's the joy of having your favourite music filling the space while you cook, or coming home from a farmers' market or greengrocer with armfuls of beautiful produce, or making yourself a pot of tea and taking the time to really enjoy a few minutes of quiet, watching the steam rise from your cup as you sip. They don't need to be grand gestures, but how you feel when you cook for yourself and those you love is your unique connection to food. No one else will be drawn to a distinctive aroma in the same way you are, or choose colours in the same way, or combine flavours in the same way; it's a private conversation between you and what you're cooking, and I love that.

Sometimes the mere fact I have food is enough to join those dots of connection for me — so the idea of being able to create with flavour and colour feels like the most amazing inspiration of my day. And then, other times, life is insanely busy and I'll eat a slice of toast for dinner and not think about any of the above. But I can tell you which meal I feel better after eating.

In the same way that I hope this book nudges plants from their often sideline status, I'd love you to see the Staple Provisions chapter for the humble star it is, and for you to make the very best use of that chapter, as it gathers all the foundational flavour tips I have garnered over the years.

EQUIPMENT

I'm not a big fan of gadgets, but there are five things I couldn't imagine not having in my kitchen these days — a set of digital scales, Vitamix, food processor, manual pasta machine and tofu press.

I started really relying on weighing ingredients using digital scales rather than cup measures when first learning to make sourdough, because no other method will give the accuracy you need in baking bread. I quickly adopted that approach to cake baking, too, as I've found that rather than messing around with measuring cups and spoons, it's easier to leave a mixing bowl on the scales and add all the ingredients by weight — including liquids. (See the intro to my Quince Hummingbird Cake recipe on page 190 for the reality-TV-style deal-clincher in favour of weighing ingredients, rather than relying on cup and tablespoon measurements, which differ from country to country.) I now weigh everything down to the smallest amounts of baking powder or salt, and that's how I'd encourage you to use the recipes in this book if possible. It will make your cooking easier and more enjoyable because you'll have great results — rather than guessing where

things went askew after the fact. I'm all for intuition in cooking, but perhaps start by getting the foundations of a recipe down pat by weighing everything, and then let your creative touch ride on top of that.

My Vitamix blender has changed the way I cook, and the staple goodies that now regularly end up in my fridge. I use it for smoothies, raw tarts, making icing for cakes, almond ricotta, blending soups, making flour blends, ice cream, dips, tofu and nut milks. There are of course other brands, and this is in no way a sponsored opinion, so do your research and invest in a quality high-speed blender that will give you extra-smooth results when it comes to processing food, in particular nuts. The price isn't to be scoffed at, but I really think it's worth it.

My food processor I use for everything else I don't do in my Vitamix: tart bases, pasta dough, gomasio, macadamia parmesan, oatcakes, nut butters — anything I want to be evenly mixed, while still retaining some texture. I mix some cakes entirely in my food processor, too.

For years I made all my sourdough-based recipes by hand. That is totally doable if you want to start making bread or buns, but don't have a stand mixer with a dough hook. Please don't think you have to wait to buy special equipment in order to have a regular rotation of baked goods being pulled from your oven. If you do end up baking sourdough more than once a week, I will be the first to say that a stand mixer makes life all that bit easier. And easier means more baking — only ever a good thing, in my mind. Even though I have a very good stand mixer with a seriously durable dough hook, I still use my sense of touch to determine when a dough is properly mixed and to check its temperature, so it's not as if having a stand mixer necessarily alters the intuitive appreciation I hope you'll develop for sourdough... but it will almost certainly save your shoulders and arms

from protesting when you next bake. I also use the whisk attachment on my stand mixer whenever I make aquafaba meringue (see page 198) — there's no way I could do that by hand!

I know fresh pasta can be rolled out by hand using a rolling pin and floured board, but I also know I wouldn't make pasta regularly if I didn't have my pasta machine. Small things can make big differences, and knowing I can pull together fresh fettuccine or ravioli without too much manual effort is a big deal, especially because I'm sure I married the champion spaghetti eater of the world.

A tofu press isn't going to be on everyone's list of kitchen essentials, and it wasn't on mine until quite recently — but as soon as I had a tofu press, I had homemade tofu. While you can get away with making tofu using a strainer lined with muslin (cheesecloth), it just won't be the same, so if you find yourself interested in making tofu at home, definitely bite the bullet and get a tofu press. You will love it, because it will help

you make tofu as you imagine it should be — which means you'll make it all the more often... and more homemade food is never a bad option. I use a traditional Japanese wooden press made from hinoki (Japanese cypress). These are relatively inexpensive to buy online or from a Japanese specialist food store.

SERVING SIZES

I find it difficult to suggest serving sizes for my recipes, because exclusively eating plants has meant I can eat a lot more — and also I'm not one to portion food based on caloric value. I pretty much eat until I'm full, and I've found that the more nutritionally dense food is, the faster my hunger is satisfied, so I tend not to worry about overeating. Except when it comes to curry. I always overeat curry, just because it tastes so good, not because I'm still hungry!

I would say most of the savoury recipes in this book serve 2–4 people, depending on whether you are having more than one course. Two very hungry people only having salad for lunch is quite a different scenario to four people eating three courses. I suppose what I'm trying to say is that this is another opportunity to really connect with what you're eating on a much deeper level, feeling whether you've had enough to eat, rather than having a rule around how much to eat. I'm all for that kind of intuitive eating. And as a plan B, you'll have leftovers for lunch tomorrow if you've made too much, or you can go for a second helping if you're still feeling peckish.

FLOUR

Because so many recipes in this book involve flour, and because I know not everyone will be making bespoke blends as the first option, here's an easy way to introduce some diversity of fibre. Wherever you would use a plain white wheat flour, try swapping in the same quantity

Fibre, my favourite food superhero!

There's nothing overly sexy about mentioning fibre here, but I am a massive fan of the stuff. There are so many great resources out there explaining all the many benefits of a fibre-rich diet; google Vanessa Kimbell, Professor Tim Spector and Dr Will Bulsiewicz, and you'll soon be looking at every mouthful of food as a potential opportunity to further increase your fibre intake. In a nutshell, the greater the diversity of fibre we consume, the healthier our gut microbiome will be — and the better we'll feel in a plethora of ways. I can attest to it.

Only plants give us fibre, and the idea is to aim to eat 30 different plants a day. But that doesn't mean we need to eat a whole cauliflower and a carrot to tally two plants — even the tiniest amount counts, with seeds, nuts, spices, herbs, fruit and vegies all adding diversity points to our daily total. That's why a green smoothie, a piece of sourdough toast made with your own flour blend, a sprinkle of gomasio on a salad for lunch, and a dinner of pasta with roasted tomato passata can have you at 30 plants without even trying.

This entire book is based on plants, so everything you cook from it will add to your fibre intake — and your gut, immune system, hormonal system, energy levels and general disposition will be singing because of it.

More plants. No punishment or restrictions, just keep adding in more of the good stuff.

of stoneground, unbleached plain white wheat flour, organic if possible. Unless otherwise mentioned on the packaging, most flour is roller-milled. As a process, roller-milling retains only the interior of the grain, without any of the nutrients and fibre from the wheat germ. Just by seeking out stoneground flour as an alternative, you will be including at least some benefits from the nutrient-rich bran and germ. It's not the ultimate choice for fibre diversity by any stretch, but it is definitely a step in the right direction when compared to roller-milled white flour. Stoneground flour will give you a more nutritionally dense option, and you won't need to change the ratio of other ingredients in any recipes you substitute it in.

For even more fibre diversity, the next flour step is using spelt, still in a simple 1:1 swap. I use an unbleached, white, stoneground spelt flour for basically everything — cakes, pasta, bread, cookies and muffins.

And then, when you really want to up your fibre diversity game, you can start blending your own Bespoke Flour Mix (see page 244). I have done bespoke flour blends with up to 15 different plants — grains, legumes, pulses, flowers, herbs, spices, even loose-leaf tea. Then all that's needed to majorly increase your daily fibre intake is a slice of sourdough.

Incremental steps that make food more delicious and exciting to cook: sounds good, doesn't it?

SUGAR

These days, I rarely use any other sugar but rapadura — an unbleached and unrefined whole cane sugar that still contains the molasses that is removed during the refining process, so it has less sucrose and a higher nutritional content than refined white sugar, including vitamin C, iron and magnesium. I'm not suggesting rapadura sugar is a health food, but it's definitely healthier

for you than refined white sugar. Rapadura gives a longer and slower release of energy into your body — and I much prefer its flavour; it tastes like toasted caramel to me.

I find it easier to buy one sugar in bulk, then only veer from that if I'm making something that won't look right if it's coloured with the darker brown tone of rapadura. Meringue and some cake icings come to mind — and in those rare cases I'll use a raw sugar because its colour is much lighter and the flavour not as pronounced. It is sometimes known as turbinado or demerara sugar.

I also make icing (confectioners') sugar from raw sugar by blitzing it in my Vitamix. Interestingly, the golden colour of raw sugar ends up white when blitzed into icing sugar, so I never really have a need to use actual white sugar at all.

You can absolutely use white sugar in any of my recipes, though, if that's what you have and prefer.

The other sugar I use is in liquid form: coconut nectar syrup. Again, this is a taste preference as much as a nutritional option. I love the flavour of coconut nectar syrup — it's buttery, somehow, with a caramel undertone. It's made by gathering fresh sap from coconut tree blossoms and concentrating it in a similar process to that used for maple syrup. In fact, maple syrup is a perfect substitute for coconut nectar syrup, if you'd prefer, as they have a very similar consistency.

COCONUT OIL

The coconut oil I use in my recipes is in solid form, not liquid. It is sometimes called extra virgin coconut oil or raw coconut oil, and is sold in jars or tubs in health food shops and the health food aisle of supermarkets. Raw coconut oil contains the meat and milk of the coconut, and although it is a solid white fat if kept below 25ºC (75ºF), it will easily melt into a liquid when warmed.

There are two types of raw coconut oil. One has a distinct coconut flavour; the other has had that flavour removed, and is referred to as 'deodorised' or 'purified'. Either version can be used in the recipes in this book, depending on how 'coconutty' you'd like a dish to taste.

OLIVE OIL

Wherever you see olive oil in this book, assume it is extra virgin olive oil. This is all I use, even in cakes and baking, because I love its flavour. We buy ours in bulk from friends who produce the most amazing grassy olive oil from their grove in Eden Valley. I use it on salads, over vegies before roasting, to dip sourdough into, and as a last-moment drizzle across pasta and soups.

You can always use a less 'punchy' oil if you'd rather not have the full flavour of extra virgin — in which case, even a basic vegetable oil such as rice bran or grapeseed might be more suitable.

SALT

There are two everyday salts in my pantry: Himalayan pink salt and Celtic sea salt, which I love for their flavour and mineral content. For everything Indian inspired, I use Himalayan pink salt, because to me that makes sense. We have Celtic sea salt on the table when we eat, mostly because it's finer and easier to pinch between fingers to pick up.

Anyone who has eaten my food will tell you I tend to under-salt dishes, so feel free to adjust for salt to suit your palate. I prefer to add less salt when I'm actually cooking, then let everyone salt to their own taste at the table.

In lieu of salt, I also love using gomasio (Japanese sesame salt). If you're wanting to cut back on salt a bit, try my Green Gomasio on page 234 — it still contains salt, but you can sprinkle it with abandon and feel you've seasoned your meal with more flavour depth and goodness than just one-dimensional salt.

If you make the scrambled tofu on page 26, I highly recommend seeking out black salt (kala namak), as it will add that distinctive sulphurous flavour we all associate with scrambled eggs.

For brining olives, I use a standard rock salt — nothing fancy.

CACAO

Am I just saying 'cocoa' with a South Australian accent, or is there an actual difference between cocoa and cacao? There *is* a difference — but nothing major. From a cooking point of view, the two are perfectly interchangeable; it's nutritionally where they differ most. I prefer raw cacao because it is less refined and therefore retains its naturally high levels of antioxidants, minerals and vitamins. This makes it especially beneficial in raw tarts or smoothies, when the heat of cooking doesn't come into play.

SUNDAY BRUNCH

Chapter One

In the country, there's still something sacred about Sundays. It's a phones-off, no-work, come-round-for-late-breakfast kind of day. It's the day bread is baked, or jam is made, or olives are picked. We fell into the lovely habit of having a big breakfast on Sundays, knowing we'd likely be too caught up in the garden, or collecting wood, or picking mushrooms, or riding horses, to stop for lunch. Brunch is always a good place to start for a social gathering with friends, as well, because there's no real structure to the menu. Everyone can bring something to contribute, and with endless pots of tea, it all just works. Brunch is one of those meals I always seek out when we're travelling, too, so lots of ideas have come home with us to be tweaked into plant-based forms, to be enjoyed time and time again.

The Best Scrambled Tofu

Serves 2–4

GLUTEN FREE
(with gluten-free bread)

400 g (14 oz) firm tofu
(not silken)

8 g (3 teaspoons)
nutritional yeast

5 g (1½ teaspoons)
ground turmeric

5 g (1 teaspoon) black
salt (kala namak), or salt
of choice

15 ml (½ fl oz) extra
virgin olive oil

Sourdough Bagels
(page 76) or toast,
to serve

mixed fresh herbs
(basil, parsley, dill,
chervil, fennel fronds),
roughly chopped,
to serve

If you're keen enough to try making your own tofu (page 236), you will find this scramble a different beast to using store-bought firm tofu — in a good way. Having said that, I still absolutely love it made with store-bought tofu. It's also something I usually make by instinct rather than adhering to any strict recipe, so please play around with it, using your favourite herbs and spices. If you can't find black salt (kala namak) don't worry too much, but you'll definitely notice the nod to eggs it gives the scramble.

We pile ours on toasted sourdough or bagels, sometimes with kale or mushrooms — sometimes with roasted tomatoes, but always with lots of fresh herbs, and always with a proper-sized pot of breakfast tea. It's great as part of a 'big breakfast', or just on its own if you're short on time but need something to get you through until lunch in that 'big protein' kind of way.

Using a potato masher, roughly mash the tofu in a bowl to resemble large 'crumbs'. The crumbs don't have to be uniform, in much the same way scrambled eggs aren't ever made up of same-sized bits.

Add the nutritional yeast, turmeric and salt and mash to mix through.

Heat the olive oil in a frying pan over medium–high heat and cook the tofu mixture, constantly moving it around in the pan using a spatula to prevent it sticking. It will only need 2–3 minutes, just to make sure it is really hot to serve.

Pile onto your choice of bagels or toast and top with a small mountain of chopped fresh herbs. Grind some black pepper over and serve straight away.

Kale on Toast

Serves 2–4

GLUTEN FREE
(with gluten-free bread)

400–500 g (14 oz–1 lb
2 oz) fresh kale (I prefer
Tuscan kale)

20 ml (½ fl oz) extra
virgin olive oil

30 g (1 oz) Wholefood
Vegie Stock Paste
(page 232)

15 ml (½ fl oz) lemon
juice

10–15 g (⅓–½ oz) Green
Gomasio (page 234)

mixed fresh herbs
(basil, parsley, dill,
chervil, fennel fronds),
roughly chopped,
to serve

freshly buttered
sourdough toast,
to serve

You might not imagine kale on toast could stand on its own as a delicious breakfast option... but it can — and it does! — with the not-so-secret addition of Wholefood Vegie Stock Paste (page 232) and Green Gomasio (page 234).

The first year we planted kale in our garden, I remember thinking we would need to come up with lots of ways to use it, because it was so prolific in its growth. I don't know what I was ever worried about. We use it in everything now, and still never seem to have enough of it, even though we plant more and more kale each year. I love its nutty flavour when pan-fried, and I don't add any water when I'm cooking it, so it stays 'springy' rather than being wilted in steam.

You can 'fillet' the kale by holding on to the thickest part of the stem at the base and running your other hand along the stem towards the top, to break the leafy part of the kale away from the super-fibrous stem. It's fine to have some stem in this dish, but it will take more time to cook — and that compromises the flash cooking you want for the leafy part of the kale to remain 'al dente'.

Strip the kale leaves from the stems (see above), discarding the stems. Roughly chop the leaves into 3–5 cm (1¼–2 in) strips.

Heat the olive oil in a frying pan over high heat. Add the stock paste and stir for a minute, using a long-handled wooden spoon (to avoid splutters when the kale is added).

Add the kale and cook, stirring, for 3–4 minutes, until tender: it may splutter a bit in the hot pan.

Remove from the heat and add the lemon juice, green gomasio and herbs. Give it all a final stir before piling onto freshly buttered sourdough toast.

Bagels with Carrot 'Smoked Salmon', Dill Cream Cheese & Capers

2 medium carrots
(220 g/7¾ oz)

TAMARI MARINADE

2 nori seaweed sheets,
torn into small pieces

250 ml (9 fl oz) water

30 ml (1 fl oz) extra
virgin olive oil

30 ml (1 fl oz) tamari
or soy sauce

10 ml (2 teaspoons)
liquid smoke

10 ml (2 teaspoons)
coconut nectar syrup,
or maple syrup

15 ml (½ fl oz) Apple
Cider Vinegar (page 178)

1–2 garlic cloves,
finely chopped

TO ASSEMBLE

120 g (4 oz) Almond
Ricotta (page 227)

8 g (¼ oz) Apple Cider
Vinegar (page 178)

4 Sourdough Bagels
(page 76), halved

1 small red onion,
thinly sliced

20 g (¾ oz) capers

a small handful of
dill sprigs

extra virgin olive oil,
for drizzling

I don't usually head down the fake meat path, but the idea of replicating smoked salmon bagels for a brunch I had for my father's birthday wasn't to be ignored. Dad loves smoked salmon, and I love my dad — so why not see what might come from a plant-based version of salmon?

Something utterly surprising was what came from that; Dad even claimed he'd prefer to eat my marinated roasted carrot dressed as salmon! I'm not sure if he was just being kind, but it really is good, and a great way to bring everyone to the table to enjoy 'common ground' food regardless.

The first time I tried this, I hand-cut the carrot with a knife and it was a bit rough, so I highly recommend using a mandoline if you have one, because it gives a more authentic look to the carrot, I mean salmon. In context with bagels, cream cheese, dill, capers and slices of red onion, it's a beautiful thing to behold. I've only ever made it for brunch to have with bagels, but I imagine it would also be delicious in a sandwich, or perhaps even stirred through a pasta with some Almond Ricotta (page 227) for creaminess.

You will need to begin this recipe the day before, to allow the carrot to marinate overnight.

Preheat your oven to 200ºC (400ºF). Roast the carrots, whole and unpeeled, for about 45 minutes, or until soft all the way through. Remove from the oven, sprinkle with salt and allow to cool.

Combine the marinade ingredients in a medium-sized container with a lid.

Slice the cooled carrots along their length into 2–3 mm (¹⁄₁₆–⅛ in) strips using a mandoline or a sharp knife. Add the carrot strips to the marinade, mixing well to coat. Seal the container and leave to marinate in the fridge overnight.

The following morning, mix the almond ricotta and vinegar to make the cream cheese. Remove the carrot strips from the marinade.

Toast the bagels and top with a generous amount of the cream cheese, followed by the carrot slices, onion, capers and dill sprigs.

Add a drizzle of extra virgin olive oil and a grind of black pepper and serve.

Tamari Mushrooms with Chervil

Serves 2–4

300–400 g (10½–14 oz)
fresh mushrooms
(I love Swiss browns
for this recipe)

25 g (1 oz) Turmeric
Butter (page 230)

15 ml (½ fl oz) tamari
or soy sauce

10 g (3 teaspoons)
roughly chopped
chervil

freshly buttered
sourdough toast or
bagels, to serve

Mushrooms are another brunch option that often get relegated to side dish status. I think they deserve better. I love mushrooms in all their guises — except soggy, so this dish is about fast-cooking the mushrooms with no additional liquid except a splash of tamari, giving them a beautiful caramelised flavour and colour.

If you've made a batch of Turmeric Butter (page 230), absolutely use that here, both in the frying pan and also on your hot toast or bagels before piling these mushrooms on top. Butter and mushrooms are made for each other, don't you think? If you haven't managed to get to the butter-making part just yet, you can easily use olive oil in the frying stage of this recipe and you'll still have an unctuous brunch ahead.

Chervil is a herb that bears no resemblance to itself in its dried form. If you don't have any fresh chervil — and might I just add how easily it grows in a pot — fresh thyme, basil, parsley or dill will work too. Any fresh herb adds aromatherapy to your breakfast.

Brush away any soil from the mushrooms. Chop the mushrooms into 1 cm (½ in) thick slices, including the stems.

Heat a frying pan over medium–high heat. Add the butter and mushrooms and stir for 2 minutes, until the mushrooms are softening but not overcooked. Add the tamari and continue stirring to ensure the mushrooms are coated. You will notice they'll soak up the tamari and take on a beautiful burnished colour.

Remove from the heat and add the chervil.

Serve immediately, either on their own with freshly buttered sourdough toast or bagels, or as part of a big breakfast with Scrambled Tofu (page 26) and Kale on Toast (page 27).

Pumpkin Bread with Homemade Mixed Spice

Makes a 20 cm (8 in) loaf;
serves 6–8

GLUTEN FREE
(with Gluten-Free
Flour Blend, page 245)

360 g (12¾ oz) pumpkin
(winter squash), peeled
and chopped

70 ml (2½ fl oz) extra
virgin olive oil

200 g (7 oz) coconut
nectar syrup
or maple syrup

15 g (½ oz) vanilla
bean paste

260 g (9¼ oz) Gluten-
Free Flour Blend
(page 245), or plain
(all-purpose) white
spelt flour

15 g (½ oz) Homemade
Mixed Spice (page 240)

7 g (1¾ teaspoons)
baking powder

3 g (¾ teaspoon)
bicarbonate of soda
(baking soda)

3 g (¾ teaspoon) salt

200 g (7 oz) walnuts,
roughly chopped

Having whole pumpkins gifted to me from friends' gardens when we moved back to the Barossa quickly made me up my pumpkin game.

Pumpkin soup, risotto and curries are some obvious ways to use up a pumpkin bounty, but eventually pumpkin bread is going to get your attention. The first time I made it, this bread went straight to the top of the list the following pumpkin season.

Toasted and served with Turmeric Butter (page 230) and a pot of tea... and all of a sudden autumn had a new signature fragrance in our house. How good does pumpkin bread smell? It's what I'll be baking whenever the time comes for us to put our house on the market.

I initially made this using my Gluten-Free Flour Blend (page 245) because I was sharing it with friends who didn't eat gluten. The next time I made it, I used spelt flour — but I actually prefer the flavour and texture using the gluten-free version, so that's the way the recipe has stayed ever since. Feel free to use either option; both of them will work.

Preheat your oven to 180°C (350°F). Line a 20 cm (8 in) x 8 cm (3¼ in) x 6 cm (2½ in) loaf (bar) tin with baking paper.

In a food processor, purée the pumpkin pieces with the olive oil until smooth. Add the coconut syrup and vanilla paste and blitz again.

In a large bowl, mix together the flour, mixed spice, baking powder, bicarbonate of soda and salt. Add to the food processor and blitz to mix through.

Pour the batter into the loaf tin. Sprinkle the walnuts over the loaf.

Bake for 50 minutes, or up to 1 hour, until a cake skewer poked into the centre of the loaf comes out dry.

Remove from the oven and leave to sit in the tin for 10 minutes, before turning out onto a wire rack to cool. This pumpkin bread will keep for 3–5 days in an airtight container.

Preserved Lemon Hummus

Makes about 400 g (14 oz)

GLUTEN FREE

40 ml (1¼ fl oz) lemon
juice

60 g (2 oz) tahini

250 g (9 oz) cooked
chickpeas, or drained
tinned chickpeas

30 ml (1 fl oz) extra
virgin olive oil, plus
extra for drizzling

30 ml (1 fl oz) water

1 Preserved Lemon
quarter (page 171),
plus 40 ml (1¼ fl oz)
of the brine and oil

2 large garlic cloves,
peeled

I wondered whether it's too predictable to have a hummus recipe in a plant-based cookbook... but then again, I eat my body weight in hummus every week, so perhaps that's reason enough for its inclusion. I actually made this as a last-minute takeaway snack to nibble on when I went to my friend Gill's house to discuss ideas for this book. I also had Sprouted Almonds (page 243) and Red Lentil Sprouts (page 242) in the fridge, so they came too — and along with a few toasted slices of Gilly's sourdough bread, we had something we both enjoyed so much I came home and added that hummus to the book.

My husband refers to Gill as his favourite chef, and I couldn't agree more — so when she said this was the best hummus she'd ever had, I didn't take that lightly. Gill and I first met when we were both working with Maggie Beer, and have been food-focused friends ever since. I couldn't have made this book without her.

The secret to good and creamy hummus is to blitz the lemon juice and tahini together first, before adding the remaining ingredients. I've never peeled the chickpeas; I'm just not that kinda girl.

Try spreading this hummus on Sourdough Bagels (page 76), or using it as a creamy base for Tamari Mushrooms (page 30) or Kale on Toast (page 27).

Using a high-speed blender, blitz the lemon juice and tahini until whipped and creamy. Add the remaining ingredients, and blitz again until smooth.

Taste for salt; I don't find I need to add any because of the saltiness of the preserved lemon.

Spread the hummus on a large plate with the back of a spoon and finish with a generous drizzle of olive oil. You can always scatter on a few sprouted almonds and/or red lentil sprouts if you have them on hand.

Dip away.

This hummus will keep for a week in an airtight container in the fridge.

Nimbu Pani Lemon Water

*Serves 2 very thirsty
people, or 4 as part of
a tea-filled brunch*

GLUTEN FREE

800 ml (28 fl oz) water

130 ml (4½ fl oz) lemon
juice (from 3–4 lemons)

15 ml (½ fl oz) rosewater

20 g (¾ oz) rapadura
sugar (optional)

ice cubes, to serve

fresh unsprayed rose
petals, to garnish
(optional)

It's amazing how many recipes can be transported home from all around
the world when you have a garden. Finding ways to use an abundance of fresh
produce in season seems to traverse cultures, and I love bringing those ideas
home to our hill.

Nimbu pani — lemon water, or lemonade as we'd call it — is a delicious
nod to our time spent in India over the years, and because we now have three
lemon trees that offer up a bounty of fruit each year, I was very happy to
discover how easy this is to make at home, and how many lemons you can
make good use of in one drink!

There are so very many variations of nimbu pani, but my favourite includes
rosewater. You can add sugar if you like, but I prefer it without, because I love
the slight sweetness of my homegrown Meyer lemons.

Again, this is not a hard and fast recipe, but more to share a lovely idea that
you can make your own when lemons are in abundance.

In a large jug, mix together the water, lemon juice and rosewater. Add sugar
to taste, if needed, stirring until it has dissolved.

Serve over ice, garnished with rose petals, if you have any to hand.

The nimbu pani is best served straight away, but you can mix it up to 24 hours
ahead. Just leave the addition of rose petals until just before serving.

Pineapple, Cucumber & Cumin Juice

Serves 2 very thirsty people, or 4 as part of a tea-filled brunch

GLUTEN FREE

450 g (1 lb) cucumber

450 g (1 lb) pineapple

1 teaspoon cumin seeds (not pre-ground powder)

This was our welcome drink at a truly stunning hotel in India, set in a very old, classically renovated fort in Udaipur. I first saw the hotel eight years before finally staying there. After I'd been anticipating our visit for so long, the hotel didn't disappoint — starting with this highly fragrant juice, brought to us on arrival. Now I can't smell freshly ground cumin without thinking of that bejewelled foyer.

This is such a favourite at the height of summer when our cucumbers are growing like crazy in the glasshouse — a slightly less bejewelled space than the hotel foyer of a former Maharaja's fort, but still a place of treasure in my mind.

Use really ripe pineapple in this juice if you can, and definitely go for an old-school type of cucumber, one with lots of seeds and aroma. It's a great way to use up any odd-looking ones! Toast the cumin seeds and grind them just before you add them to the juice; you won't believe they're any relation to their pre-ground cousin.

This is also a wonderful way to kickstart your digestion in the morning, whether you're following it up with a lazy brunch or a mid-week breakfast. Farmhouse meets Rajasthani fortress.

Run the cucumber and pineapple through a juicer and stir to mix.

Toast the cumin seeds in a dry frying pan over high heat for a minute or two, until they start to 'dance' in the bottom of the pan, and you can really smell their aroma.

Remove the seeds from the heat and grind using a mortar and pestle or spice grinder.

Pour the juice into glasses, generously sprinkle with the just-ground cumin seeds and serve.

Asparagus, Zucchini, Nori & Potato Terrine

Serves 4–6

GLUTEN FREE

420 g (15 oz) potatoes, scrubbed (I use Dutch creams, but any potato good for boiling will work, such as russet)

250 g (9 oz) zucchini (courgettes)

320 g (11 oz) asparagus

2 nori seaweed sheets

300 g (10½ oz) Almond Ricotta (page 227)

20 g (¾ oz) fresh mixed herbs, such as marjoram, parsley, dill and chervil, plus extra to serve

extra virgin olive oil, for drizzling

I first started playing around with this recipe for our restaurant in Bangkok, when I wanted to offer something just as fancy as the meat-based options on the menu at Eat Me. I'd never made terrine before, so I appreciated the help one of our chefs offered when I was trying to figure out what to put where the meat usually goes.

This terrine recipe has continued to morph and evolve, and now I love preparing it for dinner on Christmas Eve or lunch on Christmas Day. There's something about the time it takes that sets it apart as a 'special occasion' dish. I call it 'project cooking', and when I have the time, I love making food that sits in this category. Christmas is the perfect occasion to look forward to committing my afternoon to this terrine, in the same way I look forward to making panforte or ice cream, which are also on my project cooking list.

I'm all for fast meals that come together in no time throughout the week, but I also absolutely love the feeling of bringing something to the table where you can taste the time and effort involved. It's the best way of nurturing people you love, I think.

Don't let my ramblings put you off making this terrine, though. I promise it doesn't take forever to make — but you might want to choose some lovely music or a favourite podcast and have a whole pot of tea to yourself while you put it together. Time is a lovely ingredient in any cooking.

You will need to begin this terrine the day before, then all that's left on the day of your gathering is to slice it and serve with a drizzle of olive oil and some extra herbs.

Line a 20 cm (8 in) x 8 cm (3¼ in) x 6 cm (2½ in) terrine dish with baking paper, leaving enough overhang to completely wrap the top of the terrine once it's layered in the tin.

Add the whole potatoes to a saucepan, cover with cold water and bring to the boil over medium heat. Cook for 10–15 minutes, or until tender all the way through; the actual cooking time will depend on the size of your potatoes. Once cooked, remove from the saucepan and leave to cool on a plate while you prepare the other ingredients.

Mandoline the zucchini into thin lengths — you will need about 16 slices, so the recipe quantity given here allows for some breakages. I then use a flat sandwich press to quickly grill the slices for less than a minute, just to give them some colour; you can easily use a non-stick frying pan instead. The zucchini slices will cook very quickly, so keep an eye on them and remove them with a spatula, ensuring they don't break apart. Set aside until cool enough to handle.

Cut the asparagus spears to the length of your terrine tin and grill on the sandwich press, or in a flat non-stick frying pan, to colour, but don't overcook; 2–3 minutes will be plenty.

Line the base and sides of the terrine dish with the zucchini slices by placing two slices opposing each other in the terrine base, to run up each side of the tin. I start each slice in the middle of the base and slightly overlap them (see photos on page 38). The zucchini slices will contain the terrine once it is turned out, so be sure to place them in a uniform way so there are no gaps. Leave the ends of each zucchini slice overhanging the sides and lip of the tin while you build the terrine layers. Eventually you will wrap the zucchini slices around the top of the finished terrine to complete it. Sprinkle with a little salt and black pepper to season the zucchini before moving onto the potato layer.

Cut the boiled and cooled potatoes into slices about 1 cm (½ in) thick and use them to line the base and sides of the terrine, right next to the zucchini. I like to put a potato slice at each end of the terrine, too, as I find this helps when cutting the terrine for serving. Season the potato with salt and black pepper as you go.

Overlap the two nori sheets over the base and running up the side of the terrine, with enough overhang to wrap across the terrine at the top.

Spoon half the almond ricotta over the nori. Top with half the herbs and all the asparagus spears. Sprinkle with the remaining herbs, then smooth over the remaining almond ricotta.

Wrap the nori across the top of the ricotta and asparagus and gently press the layers to condense them. You will overlap the nori to contain the ricotta and asparagus mix.

Place another layer of potato slices on top of the wrapped nori sheets, to contain everything so far. Season with salt and black pepper. Finally, wrap the zucchini slices across the potato. Each zucchini slice should slightly overlap where it meets its opposite slice on top of the terrine.

Fold the overhanging baking paper across the finished terrine. Place some weights on top, such as a few tins of food, to gently compact the terrine, and leave to set in the fridge overnight.

The following day, using the baking paper to help you, pull the terrine from the terrine tin and place on a board for slicing. Drizzle with olive oil and serve each slice with fresh herbs.

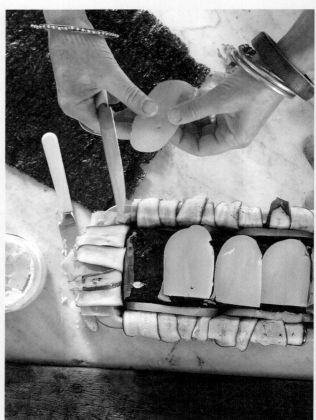

Almond Ricotta with Toasted Almonds, Lavender & Coconut Syrup

Makes about 250 g (9 oz)

GLUTEN FREE

40 g (1½ oz) raw slivered almonds

40 g (1½ oz) pistachios

200 g (7 oz) Almond Ricotta (page 227)

10 g (2½ teaspoons) vanilla bean paste

40 ml (1¼ fl oz) coconut nectar syrup

unsprayed fresh lavender flowers, to garnish

You may have guessed I love almond ricotta. Once you make it, I hope you will discover so many other ways to use it, other than those suggested in this book, but I did want to share this idea because it veers into sweet territory — rather than just thinking of ricotta as something for savoury dishes.

I put this on the brunch table so it can have fresh fruit added to it, be spread across bagels or sourdough toast and topped with roasted stone fruit or grapes, or sit next to stewed rhubarb or Poached Quinces (page 235). It also pairs deliciously with toasted Sourdough Bara Brith (page 68) or alongside Persimmon & Walnut Tea Cake (page 43).

The lavender is optional, but it makes it feel a bit fancier — and I love being able to use the flowers any way I can, because lavender grows very well on our hill. I have made this with maple syrup on many occasions too, but if you have used coconut nectar syrup in any of my other recipes, I thought you might like another reason to enjoy it. For me, it has the closest viscosity to honey, and I love the way it drizzles onto the ricotta and holds its ground.

Please don't skip toasting the nuts; it adds so much texture and fragrance to this simple idea.

To toast the nuts, place them in a single layer on a baking sheet under a moderately hot grill (broiler) for 5–8 minutes, watching them the entire time so they don't burn.

In a small bowl, mix the almond ricotta with the vanilla paste and half the coconut syrup. Spoon into a shallow bowl and drizzle with remaining coconut syrup.

Top with the toasted nuts and lavender flowers. Serve immediately.

Persimmon & Walnut Tea Cake

*Makes a 20 cm (8 in)
loaf cake; serves 6–8*

200 g (7 oz) walnuts

370 g (13 oz) plain
(all-purpose) white
spelt flour

180 g (6 oz) rapadura
sugar

3 g (¾ teaspoon) salt

3 g (¾ teaspoon)
bicarbonate of soda
(baking soda)

1 g (¼ teaspoon) baking
powder

1 g (½ teaspoon) ground
cloves

2 g (1 teaspoon) ground
cinnamon

15 g (½ oz) ground
flaxseeds (linseeds)

90 ml (3 fl oz) water

300 ml (10½ fl oz) soy
or almond milk

100 ml (3½ fl oz) extra
virgin olive oil

6 ripe, non-astringent
persimmons (look
for 'Fuyu', the most
common variety)

coconut flour, for
dusting (optional)

Persimmons were never part of my childhood in the Barossa. For me they sat in the same territory as loquats and quinces — beautiful trees and gorgeous fruit, but what to actually do with them?

I remember being handed a bag of persimmons from a generous customer at the farmers' market one Saturday morning and spending the rest of the morning asking locals what they did with them. I was told the really ripe, squashy ones can be frozen whole and scooped out with a spoon to be eaten like sorbet, the not-so-soft ones can be sliced and added to a cheeseboard or salads, and perfectly ripe ones can be treated in the same way as ripe banana and added to cakes and muffins.

I came home with an idea to combine fresh walnuts from the market that morning with the ripe, squashy persimmons to make a cake to share with Mum the following day, which was Mother's Day — and now, that's how I remember it's persimmon time. Each year ever since, I've bartered bags of tea for persimmons with friends who have trees. It's become a lovely seasonal tradition.

Preheat your oven to 180°C (350°F). Line a 20 cm (8 in) x 8 cm (3¼ in) x 6 cm (2½ in) loaf (bar) tin with baking paper.

Place half the walnuts in a mixing bowl. Add the flour, sugar, salt, bicarbonate of soda, baking powder and spices and mix together.

In a separate bowl, let the flaxseeds soak in the water until you have a thickish paste; about 3–5 minutes will do it. Stir in the milk and olive oil.

Remove the calyx from each persimmon. Roughly chop the persimmons and push through a sieve with the back of a spoon; you should end up with about 180 ml (¾ cup) of purée.

Add 125 ml (½ cup) of the persimmon purée to the flaxseed mixture and stir through, reserving the remaining purée for serving.

Add the dry ingredients to the wet ingredients and stir until completely mixed through.

Pour the batter into the loaf tin and sprinkle the remaining walnuts on top. Bake for 45–50 minutes, or until cooked through when tested with a cake skewer.

Remove from the oven and let the cake rest in the tin for 10 minutes, before turning out onto a wire rack to cool.

Dust with coconut flour, if desired. Drizzle with the remaining persimmon purée — then to the table with tea!

This tea cake will keep for 3–5 days in an airtight container. If you want to keep it in a container, only add the persimmon purée to the cake portions you will immediately eat, otherwise the purée will make the top of the cake soggy.

Blackstrap Molasses Cookies

Makes about 15

300 g (10½ oz) macadamia nuts

180 g (6 oz) rolled oats

115 g (4 oz) plain (all-purpose) white spelt flour, plus extra for rolling

110 g (3¾ oz) rapadura sugar

3 g (¾ teaspoon) bicarbonate of soda (baking soda)

3 g (1 teaspoon) ground cinnamon

180 g (6 oz) blackstrap molasses

30 ml (1 fl oz) soy or almond milk

50 ml (1¾ fl oz) extra virgin olive oil

8 g (2 teaspoons) vanilla bean paste

140 g (5 oz) sultanas (golden raisins)

While biscuits are not traditional breakfast fare, these cookies became just that for quite a few early morning Barossa Farmers' Market goers, myself included, when I had a stall there for many years. The stall was like a pop-up cafe for a while there, with regulars catching up with each other while they munched on cookies and sipped tea I shared from multiple thermoses. I would often be asked for the cookies recipe, and always joked that I'd put it in my cookbook one day. Best keep my word!

I don't bake cookies very often — not because I don't like them, but because I really like them. In my mind, though, these aren't a typical cookie. They're a bit more rustic and definitely have some elements of recognisable nutrition in their ingredients: oats, sultanas, macadamias, spelt and their namesake, blackstrap molasses. If you haven't tried blackstrap molasses before, expect a deeper, more richly flavoured version of molasses — one that is loaded with iron, too. See? Good for you.

These cookies can be prepared using a food processor, which makes life very easy. They're so delicious with tea, and also a great cookie to use for ice cream sandwiches.

Preheat your oven to 180°C (350°F) and line a baking tray with baking paper.

Put the macadamias in a food processor. Add half the oats, as well as the flour, sugar, bicarbonate of soda and cinnamon. Blitz until you have a texture similar to breadcrumbs.

Add the molasses, milk, olive oil and vanilla paste and blitz again.

This mix tends to be on the sticky side, so have an extra bowl of spelt flour ready to roll the cookie balls in before placing them on the baking tray.

Tip the dough into a bowl and incorporate the sultanas and remaining oats, leaving them whole for texture.

Gently roll heaped spoonfuls of the dough into a ball in the flour, then flatten onto the baking tray. Leave space around each cookie, so they can expand a bit when they're baking. You should end up with about 15 cookies.

Bake for 12–15 minutes, until slightly puffed up; the cookies will appear soft. Remove from the oven and leave to cool on a wire rack to crisp up a little on the outside, leaving the middle soft and chewy. These cookies will last for a week in an airtight container.

Sourdough Chocolate &
Black Tahini Babka

*Makes a 20 cm (8 in)
babka; serves 6–8*

150 g (5½ oz) sourdough
starter (see Language
of Sourdough, page 54),
fed the night before
with 100 g/3½ oz each
flour and water

180 ml (6 fl oz) water

60 ml (2 fl oz) extra
virgin olive oil, plus
extra for the bowl

50 g (1¾ oz) rapadura
sugar

450 g (1 lb) plain
(all-purpose) white
spelt flour, plus extra
for kneading

5 g (1 teaspoon) salt

CHOCOLATE
TAHINI MIX

80 g (2¾ oz) black tahini

100 g (3½ oz) dairy-free
dark chocolate drops

50 g (1¾ oz) rapadura
sugar

When we lived in Melbourne, I loved going to the bakeries in St Kilda that
had beautiful babkas lined up like fancy handbags in their windows. Always
in awe of the time and effort that obviously went into each loaf, I filed babkas
in the 'professional bakers only' archive in my mind — until I started baking
sourdough. That was the first domino to fall from the 'tricky baking' basket.
When my husband requested a 'birthday babka' instead of a cake, I took on the
challenge, thinking I'd surely need to make it a few times before I got it right.
Nope. It actually looks far more difficult than it is... and how much do we love
recipes like that?

   This is not a traditional babka in any shape or form — firstly because it's
sourdough, secondly because it's plant-based, and finally because in my mind
it's not complicated enough to be deemed an authentic babka. In truth, this is
my sourdough hot cross bun recipe, which I turned into my Plaited Sourdough
Spiced Buns recipe on page 72, and here is also happy to dress itself up in
chocolate and black tahini.

   Slices of this babka can be toasted in a sandwich press the next day, but it is
so much better straight from the oven. I love making this when we have friends
come to stay, because I can split the process over two days, and we can all enjoy
freshly baked babka on Sunday morning.

   If you'd like to bake the babka first thing Sunday morning, you will need
to start this recipe by feeding your starter on a Friday night, with 100 g (3½ oz)
flour and 100 ml (3½ fl oz) water.

To make the dough, combine the sourdough starter, water, olive oil and sugar
in a large bowl. I use my Kitchen Aid for the dough mixing, but it can be done
by hand, too.

Add the flour and salt to the wet mixture. If you're using a mixer with a dough
hook, you will only need to mix for 3–4 minutes. If working by hand, knead
the dough on the bench for 8–10 minutes, until smooth and elastic, then place
the kneaded dough back in the bowl.

Cover the bowl with plastic wrap or a silicone cover and leave at room
temperature for 6–8 hours, until the dough has doubled in volume.

Once doubled in size, roll the dough out into a 40 cm (16 in) square, about 5 mm
(¼ in) thick. Don't worry too much if it isn't a perfect square; the dough will
figure itself out during baking.

Mix the black tahini and rapadura sugar together in a small bowl. Spread the
mixture across the square of dough, leaving a 1–2 cm (½–¾ in) border around
the edges. Scatter the chocolate drops across the surface and gently press them
into the tahini, so they don't fall about when you roll the babka.

To shape the babka, start with the edge closest to you. Roll the dough away from you, using both hands to keep it as tightly rolled as you can. If some of the filling pushes towards the edges, don't worry too much — just wash your hands if things get too messy!

At this point, I turn the dough roll so it is running end to end towards me. (I find it easier to gauge the middle of the roll this way.) Using a very sharp knife, cut right along the middle of the entire length of the dough log. You will end up with two half-moon lengths of filled dough, hopefully with the open layers facing up. If the two lengths are not facing upwards to contain the filling, turn them so they are. You'll need them both to have their dough 'bottoms' on the bench for the next step.

With the two dough lengths running right next to each other, take one length and gently place it over the other, continuing to braid the dough lengths until they are completely wrapped around each other. Keep the open layers facing up at all times.

Place the dough in a loaf (bar) tin lined with baking paper, gently compacting it to fit. Cover and leave in the fridge to slowly prove overnight.

Next morning, remove the loaf tin from the fridge and bring up to room temperature while your oven is heating to 220°C (425°F). (I put my babka tin on top of my stove while the oven is heating up, to help warm up the dough.)

Place the babka in the oven and immediately reduce the temperature to 200°C (400°F). Bake for 40–50 minutes, until beautifully burnished.

Remove from the oven and leave to cool on a wire rack before slicing. The babka will keep for 3–5 days in an airtight container.

Stovetop Chai

Serves 2–4

GLUTEN FREE

20 g (¾ oz) looseleaf
Darjeeling tea

2 cm (¾ in) thick slice
of fresh ginger, halved

2 x 8 cm (3¼ in) lengths
of cinnamon bark

4 cardamom pods,
slightly crushed

4 cloves

4 black peppercorns

½ teaspoon fennel
seeds

400 ml (14 fl oz) water

400 ml (14 fl oz) soy or
almond milk

coconut nectar syrup
or palm sugar (jaggery),
to taste

There is a very big difference between a chai tea bag hurriedly dunked in water, and the ritual of mixing spices and looseleaf tea to brew on the stovetop. You've probably guessed I'm going to advocate for the latter. Wholeheartedly. I have so many lovely memories of having chai with friends on cold afternoons, near the fire, here at our farmhouse.

In the times we've visited India, our travel has been punctuated by drinking chai on dusty roads en route to the next little town, in sellers' houses while we looked at handmade wares, at quick pit stops where we walked out with hot chapati in one hand and a terracotta cup of chai in the other — but without a doubt, the most incredible chai-based experience I have ever had was at a monastery in the Himalayas, where we were invited into the huge kitchen with walls blackened by 700 years of cooking, and watched as a monk brewed up a small bath full of chai for his 80 fellow resident monks. The only light coming in was through the tiniest sliver of a window, making the cooking flames all the more dramatic in contrast, with the whole scene set to the soundtrack of low, rumbling chanting in the temple adjoining the kitchen, as the chai was stirred with what looked like the paddle of a row boat in a giant cauldron. So amazing. It really showed what an awe-inspiring ritual making tea can be. Let's never speak of tea bags again.

Fill a 1 litre (35 fl oz) teapot with just-boiled water, to heat the teapot while you prepare the chai.

Place all the ingredients, except the milk and sugar, in a medium-sized saucepan and bring to the boil over high heat.

Allow the brew to boil for only 1–2 minutes — long enough to extract the flavour from the spices, but not so long that the tannins from the tea override all the other ingredients.

Add the milk and heat through, removing the pan from the stove as soon as you see the chai just begin to boil again.

If you'd like to add sweetener, stir it through the chai to dissolve it before straining the tea into your warm teapot for serving.

That smell! The best.

SOURDOUGH

Chapter Two

When we first moved back to the Barossa, whenever I'd visit Sydney I would bring home loaves of sourdough from Bourke Street Bakery to put in our freezer, because at the time local bakeries weren't making it. Too hard, too unreliable, too slow was what I heard from bakers. Sourdough was a necessity for us, so after a while I tracked down a master in William Wood from Carême Pastry — right here in the Barossa. William had been tinkering with a sourdough starter a chef had brought back from San Francisco. Through a process akin to the 'Chinese whispers' of breadmaking, we learnt everything we knew from William after hours in his back kitchen. William had a 'secret' sourdough club that really wasn't very secret at all. People on the list would receive a message he was baking on a given day, and they'd come down the back lane into the shed to pick up their still-warm bread. 'You guys should get something going at the markets' were the only words we needed from Will, and soon enough we were baking up to 200 loaves a week for our community. It made us feel like rock stars!

As you'll see in this chapter, once you have a sourdough starter, you'll be able to have a wonderful range of goods on your table besides bread.

the language of sourdough

The art of making sourdough is only half the story
to a successful loaf; the other part lies in understanding
the language that accompanies the craft. It can be
a bit tricky to wrap your head around 'mothers' and
'starters' when you first contemplate sourdough baking,
so here's a handy go-to guide to refer to along the way,
should things get a bit curly.

MOTHER / STARTER

A sourdough 'mother' — also known as the 'starter' — is where it all begins. This is the actual mixture of flour and water that contains the living culture that creates the activity that enables a dough to rise prior to baking. This starter culture is full of the wild yeasts and bacteria unique to your environment. You will need to feed the mother with water and flour to provide the habitat for the microbes to exist.

WHERE DO I GET A MOTHER / STARTER?

While there are many references online to making your own starter, I will be super honest in saying I think you will get a better result from acquiring a small amount of sourdough starter from a friend who bakes sourdough, or asking a local bakery if you can please buy some active starter. With so many people baking sourdough these days, I'm sure you can think of someone who might share their starter with you, especially considering it is a waste product at certain stages of the sourdough process, and likely to be thrown away otherwise.

If you've been making sourdough for a while and would like to experiment with making your own starter, go ahead and check out some online instructions... but for those embarking on the sourdough journey for the first time, having an established starter — with an active microbial culture ready and raring to go — will give the best chances of early success. And I really want you to have success when you first try baking a loaf, so you love it, and you'll continue to further immerse yourself in the amazing alchemy that is sourdough baking.

DO I REALLY HAVE TO WEIGH EVERYTHING ON SCALES, RATHER THAN USE CUP MEASUREMENTS?

The simple answer here is yes. And the reason is two-fold. Firstly, you can be sure to get a consistent result with your breadmaking if you have accurate amounts of ingredients each time — and this can only be done by weight, because my cup of flour might be grams away from yours. The second reason to weigh everything — including water — is for ease. Once you have your mixing bowl or container of mother on your digital scales, you can tare the scales and then leave the bowl there to weigh the flour, water and salt, without any back and forth. This is a super-important part of the process — please don't 'guesstimate' when it comes to baking!

HOW DO I FEED THE MOTHER / STARTER?

When you first receive your mother, keep it in a large glass jar (or non-reactive container), at least 750 ml (26 fl oz) in capacity. I have mine in an enamel container with a lid, which I keep in the fridge between feeds. When I am going to bake, I remove my container from the fridge and let the mother come to room temperature on the kitchen bench for a few hours before feeding it. I feed my starter around 8 pm the night before I mix my loaf, so it has time to become active before I add it to my bread ingredients.

You want your starter to be recently fed with water and the same flour you'll use in your loaf. You don't want to use a starter that has eaten all of the available food, and is therefore no longer as active — this is known as a 'spent' starter.

I bake at least twice a week, so I don't need to *double-feed* my starter before I mix my bread, but for those who are baking only once a week or less, I recommend the following...

Remove the starter container from the fridge at 3 pm the day before you mix your bread. Remove half of the starter and discard (or place in a separate jar if you want to save your spent starter to use in the granola on page 67, for example). Using scales to weigh all your ingredients, add 50 g (1¾ oz) water and 50 g (1¾ oz) flour to the remaining starter and mix thoroughly with a spatula or spoon. Leave for 3–4 hours on the benchtop at room temperature.

At 8 pm, again remove half of the starter (and either discard, or add to your saved jar of spent starter). Feed the remaining starter with 100 g (3½ oz) water and 100 g (3½ oz) flour. Mix thoroughly and leave on the benchtop at room temperature overnight. This will be your 'active' starter to add to your bread ingredients the following morning.

The next morning, once you have added the required amount of active starter to your bread ingredients (each recipe will tell you how much you need), you can feed the remaining starter with 50 g (1¾ oz) each of water and flour, then keep in the fridge until you next bake. This way you can keep the starter active, without having to feed it every day and waste lots of flour.

HOW OFTEN DO I NEED TO FEED THE MOTHER / STARTER?

This will depend entirely on how often you bake. I prefer to use what I call the 'hungry mother' method, which is all about feeding just before baking, rather than feeding every day. In between baking, I keep the mother in the same enamel container, in the fridge, unfed.

When I'm going to bake for the first time after removing the mother from the fridge, I bring the mother up to room temperature, discard half, then feed the rest with 50 g (1¾ oz) water and 50 g (1¾ oz) flour. After 3–4 hours on the benchtop, I again discard half the starter, feed the rest with 100 g (3½ oz) water and 100 g (3½ oz) flour, then leave the starter out of the fridge overnight, ready to mix my bread the following morning.

If I've already made a loaf of bread and decide to bake sourdough buns the following day, I simply leave my starter out of the fridge, feed it with 100 g (3½ oz) water and 100 g (3½ oz) flour, leave it on the benchtop overnight and then mix the buns the next morning. I only do a 'double-feed and discard' if it's the first time I've baked for the week. If my starter has been fed and is active because I've already made bread, then there's no need to double-feed the starter, or to discard any, because it's ready to go from the day before.

MY WEEKLY SOURDOUGH ROUTINE

More often than not, my routine is to bake buns on a Friday, and then bake bread on a Saturday, so my weekly plan goes like this...

- Wednesday afternoon: Take the starter from the fridge, bring to room temperature, discard half and feed the rest with 50 g (1¾ oz) water and 50 g (1¾ oz) flour. Leave for 3–4 hours, discard half the starter again, and feed the rest with 100 g (3½ oz) water and 100 g (3½ oz) flour. Leave the fed starter out of the fridge overnight.
- Thursday morning: Mix the buns, then leave in the fridge overnight to bake on Friday. Leave the starter on the benchtop all day Thursday.
- Thursday night: Around 8 pm, feed the starter 100 g (3½ oz) water and 100 g (3½ oz) flour. Leave the fed starter out of the fridge, ready to mix into my bread next day.
- Friday morning: Bake my buns. Mix my bread, to leave in the fridge overnight and bake the next day.
- Saturday morning: Bake the bread.

WHAT IS THE 'FLOAT' TEST?

This is one of the best tips I could possibly share when it comes to sourdough baking. It is also one of the simplest. We like those!

To tell whether your fed starter is ready to be added to the remaining ingredients when mixing a loaf of bread, simply weigh the amount of water for your loaf into the mixing bowl first, followed by the amount of starter specified in the recipe. If the starter floats on the water, you can continue weighing the rest of the ingredients into the bowl for your loaf of bread.

If the starter doesn't float, at least you haven't wasted all the ingredients on a loaf that would most likely be a flop. Instead, simply discard the water and starter in the bowl, and feed the mother again with 100 g (3½ oz) flour and 100 g (3½ oz) water. You will lose a day waiting for the starter to be ready to float-test again — but when you have visual confirmation that your starter is aerated and good to go, you know you'll end up with a delicious finished loaf.

WHAT IS 100% HYDRATION?

'Hydration' is the term given to the amount of water (in comparison to flour) when we feed our starter. If we add 50 g (1¾ oz) water and 50 g (1¾ oz) flour, this is known as 100% hydration. If we add 100 g (3½ oz) water and 100 g (3½ oz) flour, this is also 100% hydration. If the amount of water and flour (in grams) is the same, then you are working with 100% hydration.

All the sourdough recipes in this chapter work with 100% hydration for the starter. Hydration in reference to the mixing of a final loaf is another thing...

What is hydration when referred to in a recipe, rather than in relation to feeding a starter?

I told you things can get curly in the world of sourdough! Okay, so once we've added our fed starter (100% hydration) to our other bread ingredients, bakers will often refer to the overall hydration of the loaf. In this case, they are talking about the amount of water to flour, as a percentage of the finished loaf.

So, if we've added 750 g (1 lb 10 oz) water and 1000 g (2 lb 4 oz) flour to 200 g (7 oz) of starter (100% hydration), then the overall hydration of the loaf is 75% — because 750 g (1 lb 10 oz) water is 75% of the 1000 g (2 lb 4 oz) flour in the loaf.

I really hope that makes sense. If not, you really don't need to worry too much about it. The main hydration reference to get right is the one relating to feeding the starter, and in my recipes it's always 100% — the same amount of water as flour.

WHAT WATER SHOULD THE MOTHER DRINK?

To ensure the mother stays active, it's best to use filtered water or rainwater, at room temperature. Tap water contains chlorine, which can destroy the active microbial culture in your starter over time.

WHAT FLOUR SHOULD I FEED THE MOTHER WITH?

Whatever flour you decide to make your bread with, is the flour you should feed your starter.

If you are making a bread using 100% unbleached white wheat flour, feed your starter with unbleached white wheat flour.

If you decide to replace 10% (or 100 g/3½ oz) unbleached white wheat flour with 100 g (3½ oz) of the Bespoke Flour Mix on page 244, you should still feed your starter with unbleached white wheat flour, because this will still be the main flour in the loaf.

If you want to experiment with 50% rye flour and are happy to have a heavier loaf, then you might like to separate your starter into two containers, and incrementally feed one starter with rye flour rather than white flour. Do this over three or four feeds so you don't 'shock' the starter, but it will definitely help to create the perfect environment for the microbes that will activate the rye flour. That way, your rye bread won't be as heavy, because there will be more microbes feeding on rye rather than white wheat.

DO I HAVE TO WAIT ALL NIGHT FOR MY STARTER TO BECOME ACTIVE?

Again, the simple answer is yes. Sourdough is a slow food. The longer the proving process for bread, the easier it is for us to digest, because the microbes are doing some of the work for us on that front. Plus, I'd argue that the slower the process, the more delicious the bread is — and the more we'll appreciate it! You'll know when the starter is ready because the float test will confirm the activity for you. Don't skip that step; it makes all the difference.

WHAT FLOUR SHOULD I DUST MY WRAPPING CLOTH WITH?

Everyone loves that beautiful contrast of flour on a perfectly burnished loaf of bread — but you don't want to risk drying out your loaf by loading it up with flour that will only get absorbed by the dough and disappear once it is baked anyway.

The answer is to use a starchy flour. This won't be absorbed, so you'll see it on the finished loaf, and it's also fantastic to help prevent dough sticking to the wrapping linen while it's proving overnight. I use arrowroot flour when I'm shaping and wrapping my dough. You can also use white rice flour (not brown rice flour) or tapioca.

I keep a jar of arrowroot flour on the kitchen bench where I shape and wrap my dough, so I know it's always within reach.

DO I NEED A PROPER BREAD BASKET (BANNETON) TO MAKE SOURDOUGH?

You may want to add a banneton to your wish list, but by no means let its absence stop you from baking bread. I use an enamel colander — and although we have two different-shaped bannetons, I actually prefer the shape I get from using my colander.

Sourdough Bread

Makes a 2 kg (4 lb 8 oz) loaf

DAY 1

Sourdough starter (see Language of Sourdough, page 54)

50 g (1¾ oz) filtered water, at room temperature, plus another 100 g (3½ oz) filtered water

50 g (1¾ oz) plain (all-purpose) unbleached white wheat flour, plus another 100 g (3½ oz) flour

DAY 2

200 g (7 oz) fed sourdough starter (from Day 1, above)

750 g (1 lb 10 oz) filtered water, at room temperature

25 g (1 oz) salt, finely ground

1 kg (1 lb 2 oz) plain (all-purpose) unbleached white wheat flour

arrowroot flour or white rice flour, for dusting

Sourdough is not something only those with time on their hands can make. This no-knead method can easily become a regular part of your weekly routine, even if said routine is crazy busy. I break this recipe down across three days so it's not as overwhelming; the idea is to start two days before you would like to bake, and you will have fresh bread on the third day. I usually begin on a Thursday night, feeding my starter before I go to bed, then mixing my loaf on Friday, and baking it to have fresh bread for Saturday morning. I can absolutely assure you, once you've done this a few times, you won't even think about it as something you need to set aside huge amounts of time for. You'll be too busy thinking about all the other sourdough things you can make.

Sourdough is the best kind of alchemical adventure — start now is always my advice. I can't tell you how many people have made absolute cracking loaves on their first attempt using this method, quickly followed by, 'I don't know what I was so scared of!'

Remember to weigh all your ingredients, even the water.

DAY 1

Take your sourdough starter (also known as the 'mother') from the fridge and bring to room temperature. Discard half the starter, to ensure a portion of the 'spent' starter that has exhausted its food source is removed, retaining the remaining starter for its microbial population.

Feed the remaining starter with 50 g (1¾ oz) filtered room-temperature water and 50 g (1¾ oz) flour (using the same type of flour you'll be using in your actual loaf). To do this, simply mix the flour and water into the starter and leave on the benchtop at room temperature for 3–4 hours.

Discard half the starter again, and this time feed the remaining starter with 100 g (3½ oz) filtered water and 100 g (3½ oz) flour. Cover and leave on the bench overnight, to use in your bread tomorrow.

DAY 2

Set a large mixing bowl over your digital scales, so you can accurately measure all your ingredients as they are added to the bread dough.

Check your starter is ready by doing the 'float' test. Pour 750 (1 lb 10 oz) room-temperature filtered water into your mixing bowl, then add 200 g (7 oz) of the fed starter — it should float on the surface of the water, not sink to the bottom of the bowl. If it passes, you're good to go. If it does sink, don't panic — simply feed the starter with another 100 g (3½ oz) water and 100 g (3½ oz) flour that

TOOLS OF THE TRADE

25–30 cm (10–12 in) cast-iron ovenproof casserole dish with lid (I use Le Creuset)

razor blades for scoring bread

linen cloth, about 40 cm (16 in) square

baking paper

large bowl

rubber spatula

digital scales (non-negotiable! See Language of Sourdough, page 54)

20 cm (8 in) bread basket or colander

night, and run the process again the following morning. You'll be a day behind, but at least you won't waste your efforts on bread that won't bake well without a healthy starter.

When your starter is floating in the water, stir gently to break up the starter into the water. Add 25 g (1 oz) salt and stir again. Add 1 kg (1 lb 2 oz) white flour and stir by hand with a rubber spatula, making sure all the liquid has been incorporated and there are no pockets of dry flour. Cover and leave for 30 minutes on the bench at room temperature.

After 30 minutes, use the spatula to 'fold' the bread by sliding the spatula down between the dough and the bowl and gently pulling the dough up over the top of itself. Turn the bowl by a quarter and repeat until all four quarters have been folded over the top of the dough. Cover and leave for another 30 minutes on the bench at room temperature.

Repeat the folding every 30 minutes, another three times, over the next 1½ hours.

Cover the dough and leave to rise for 3–4 hours, until it has increased by at least one-third in volume. This may take longer, depending on the ambient room temperature.

When the dough has risen, you are ready to wrap it and leave to prove further in the fridge overnight. Very gently turn the dough out onto a floured board; I use a starchy flour, like arrowroot or white rice flour, because it doesn't stick, and it doesn't get absorbed into the dough, which would make it dry.

Fold each side of the dough in over itself, almost like an envelope. You don't want to lose those lovely bubbles of air trapped in the dough, so while this process needs to be done quickly, you also want to be as gentle as possible in the handling.

Flip the loaf so the seam is facing down and leave for 10–20 minutes to seal the seam.

Light dust your linen cloth with flour, then use it to line your bread basket (or colander, in my case). To get the loaf into the cloth-lined basket or colander, use a dough slide to lift and flip the dough so it lands with the seam facing upwards in the basket. Wrap the cloth snugly around the loaf, tucking it in down the sides, so no parts of the loaf are exposed to the air.

Place the wrapped loaf in its basket in the fridge overnight.

DAY 3

Take the loaf from the fridge and leave in the basket or colander to come to room temperature while you heat your oven and cast-iron casserole dish.

Turn your oven right up. Mine only goes to 220°C (425°F), but you want your oven as hot as possible. Place the empty casserole dish, with its lid on, in the oven. You may need to adjust the shelves in your oven to give yourself enough room, remembering you'll need to remove the very hot lid throughout the cooking stage. I have plenty of baker's scars to prove this is worth getting right!

Once your oven is up to at least 200°C (400°F), prepare the loaf for baking by having a 25 cm (10 in) square of baking paper ready, as well as your razor blade for making the cuts on top of your bread. The next part has to happen reasonably quickly, so make sure you have everything at hand, rather than scrambling at the last minute.

Take the hot casserole dish out of the oven and have it standing by.

Unwrap the top of the linen cloth and place the baking paper over the dough. With one hand holding the paper against the loaf, use your other hand to flip the loaf out onto the board and remove the cloth. Quickly score the top of the bread with the razor blade.

Remove the hot lid of the dish. Pick the loaf up by using opposing corners of the baking paper to lower it down into the hot pan. This can get ouchy if you're not concentrating, so don't attempt to Instagram in this moment!

Place the lid back on the dish and place in the oven to cook for 45 minutes. Set a timer so you don't go out to water the garden and find the runner ducklings have hatched... and although that's a lovely thing, your three days of effort in the bread-baking stakes have turned to charcoal. Just saying.

After 45 minutes, remove the lid and bake for a further 15–20 minutes, depending on how burnished you like the crust. I always go for 20 minutes. (If your oven is still sitting higher than 220°C/425°F after losing heat opening the door to put the bread back in, you can knock the temperature back a touch so it sits at 220°C/425°F.)

Once your loaf is cooked, remove the dish from the oven and turn the bread out onto a cooling rack. It's best not to cut it until it has completely cooled, otherwise you'll squash slices rather than cut them. But I've done that too.

Enjoy your bread. It will be the most amazing bread you've ever eaten — the taste of serious self-satisfaction. Be prepared to become one of those sourdough-obsessed people who leave parties early because they have to get home to feed their mother. I'm super excited for you!

Sourdough Cardamom Breakfast Buns

Makes 8 buns

DAY 1

Sourdough starter (see Language of Sourdough, page 54)

100 g (3½ oz) plain (all-purpose) unbleached white wheat flour

100 g (3½ oz) filtered water, at room temperature

DAY 2

150 g (5½ oz) fed sourdough starter (from Day 1, above)

75 g (2½ oz) extra virgin olive oil

210 g (7½ oz) soy or almond milk

100 g (3½ oz) rapadura sugar

5 g (1 teaspoon) salt

1 g (1 teaspoon) ground cardamom

3 g (2 teaspoons) fennel seeds

2 g (4 teaspoons) crushed dried rose petals (optional)

400 g (14 oz) unbleached plain (all-purpose) spelt flour, plus extra for rolling

We live far enough away from any supermarket that I really think twice before I get in the car to make the trek. Bakeries fall into the same category. Plus, although I can just as easily get lured in by shiny things in bakery cabinets as the next tea drinker, I actually prefer something a little more rustic than what is generally found for sale on those shelves.

I love baked goods to have prettiness about them, to really give you that evocative feeling of having something special to enjoy with a pot of tea, but at the same time, I love tasting all the individual ingredients — not just a tsunami of sugar. Give me spelt flour and brown sugar and punches of spice any time — all the better if it's sourdough.

I think it's the way these rolled buns show off the almond butter filling in their gorgeous twists and folds that initially made me fall in love with them when I first pulled them from the oven... but it was the fact I had another use for my sourdough mother that made these part of my weekly baking. Along with the sourdough bagels (page 76) and muffins (page 79), these buns make sure I don't waste any of the feeds I give my sourdough starter throughout the week, in between baking actual loaves. It's great to have a few other options for making full use of your sourdough starter; that way, your starter is always active, and you'll be enjoying other naturally leavened delights besides bread. Pulling warm baked buns fresh from the oven around 10.30 am seems like common sense to me.

Remember to weigh all your ingredients, even the liquids.

DAY 1

Take your sourdough starter from the fridge and bring to room temperature. Discard half the starter, to ensure a portion of the 'spent' starter is removed. Feed your starter by mixing in the flour and water and leave on the benchtop at room temperature overnight.

DAY 2

Mix the fed sourdough starter, olive oil and milk in a large bowl. Add the sugar, salt, cardamom, fennel seeds and rose petals (if using), and stir through. Finally, add the flour in increments, making sure it is all incorporated evenly throughout the dough, with no dry flour pockets.

Knead the dough for 3–5 minutes by hand on the bench; if using a stand mixer with a dough hook, you'll only need to mix for 2–3 minutes to incorporate all the ingredients. Leave in the bowl, cover and place somewhere warm for 2–3 hours, until increased in size by one-third.

ALMOND BUTTER FILLING

60 g (2 oz) Turmeric Butter (page 230), fridge cold

60 g (2 oz) rapadura sugar

40 g (1½ oz) almond meal

zest of 2 oranges

8 g (2 teaspoons) vanilla bean paste

1 g (1 teaspoon) ground cardamom

Blitz all the filling ingredients in a food processor for 20–30 seconds — or in a bowl — until the mixture is blended but still has texture. Cover and place in the fridge until needed.

Once the dough has risen, roll it out on a floured surface, to about 60 cm (24 in) long and 40 cm (16 in) wide, keeping the long side closest to you. It should end up 3–5 mm (⅛–¼ in) thick. Spread the filling over the dough, leaving a clear 1 cm (½ in) border along the edges. Take the top half of the dough and gently, but decisively, flip it over the lower half, sandwiching the almond butter inside.

Working from the top of the longest side of the rectangle, to the bottom of the longest side closest to you, use a sharp knife to cut the dough in half towards you, into two large rectangles. Now cut each rectangle in half again, from the top to the bottom, giving four smaller rectangles in total. Slice each rectangle in half again, from top to bottom, into quarters, and finally into eight long, thin pieces.

Leaving a 2 cm (¾ in) space at the top of each strip, cut down along the middle all the way to the end, to create two strips that are still joined at the top — like a pair of trousers.

Take the left-hand strip and twist it outwards to the left, then take the right-hand strip and twist it outwards to the right. Keep twisting until the dough won't take anymore tension, about four or five twists each side. Then, taking a strip in each hand, twist the two lengths in on themselves to resemble a knot, and tuck in the ends (see photos on pages 64–65). Don't overthink this, or it will become all the more tricky. Just let your hands figure it out, and regardless of how your knots come together, they will look beautiful once baked — trust me!

Place the buns on a baking tray lined with baking paper, leaving 2–3 cm (¾–1¼ in) between each to allow for rising. Cover and leave in the fridge overnight to prove.

DAY 3

Next morning, take the buns from the fridge and let them come to room temperature while your oven heats to 200°C (400°F).

Bake for 20–25 minutes, until golden brown and smelling like a Moroccan spice market. Some of the butter will ooze out of the buns and pool around their bases — this is all part of the tradition of these buns, so embrace it!

Pop the kettle on. Time for freshly baked buns.

Once cooled, the buns will keep in an airtight container for 2–3 days. Warm them using a sandwich press or air-fryer for a few minutes before eating.

Sourdough Granola with Sesame, Macadamia & Dried Figs

Makes about 1.5 kg
(3 lb 5 oz)

280 g (10 oz) sourdough starter (fed within the previous 2 days; see Language of Sourdough, page 54)

200 g (7 oz) maple syrup

60 g (2 oz) extra virgin olive oil

40 g (1½ oz) vanilla bean paste

380 g (13½ oz) rolled oats

280 g (10 oz) macadamia nuts

220 g (7¾ oz) sesame seeds

10 g (2½ teaspoons) Homemade Mixed Spice (page 240)

3 g (¾ teaspoon) salt

280 g (10 oz) dried figs, chopped

So, this is a little left field, but it's also delicious, and it's the thing I do when I've fed my starter the night before, fully intending to make a loaf of sourdough the next day, but my plans are hijacked and I can't make bread... and I don't want to waste the starter. If you find yourself in a similar position at some point, why not let homemade granola be the answer?

I've never liked cereal in a box, but the first time I came across homemade granola in all its toasty glory, it felt like I'd just discovered fresh asparagus after only ever having tinned. It's a marked difference, and absolutely worth the minimal effort involved — especially if you make a big batch (double the recipe below), then store it in jars to enjoy over several weeks.

Feel free to replace the dried figs with other fruit; I've made this with dried apricots, goji berries, pears and apples — all are really good. Likewise for the nuts. We dehydrate a batch of figs each year when we can't keep up with eating them fresh, so I always have those on hand. Just take this recipe as a base guideline for you to play with. The main point is that you have a Plan B for sourdough starter looking for a purpose in its life.

On that note, if you'd like to use starter that hasn't been fed for a while, you can certainly do that; you will just have a more pronounced sourdough flavour in your finished granola. Or you can feed your starter the night before, as you would if you were going to make bread. No complaints either way.

Remember to weigh all your ingredients, even the liquids.

Preheat your oven to 180°C (350°F).

In a large bowl, mix together the sourdough starter, maple syrup, olive oil and vanilla paste. The sourdough starter can still have a few lumps — it will figure itself out in the baking.

Add the oats, macadamias, sesame seeds, mixed spice and salt. Mix through to ensure no dry pockets remain.

Pour the granola mixture onto a lined baking tray (or two trays, if doubling the recipe), using your fingers to gently push the granola into a roughly even layer.

Bake for 20 minutes, then remove the tray from the oven and turn the granola over as best you can using tongs or a large spoon. Bake for a further 20 minutes, or until nicely toasted.

Remove from the oven and allow to cool completely before adding the dried figs.

Store the granola in an airtight jar in the pantry. If you'd like to keep it for up to a month, think about only adding the dried fruit just before you serve it. Keeping the dried fruit separate will retain the crunch in the granola for much longer.

Sourdough Bara Brith

Makes two 20 cm (8 in) loaves

DAY 1

Sourdough starter (100% hydration; see Language of Sourdough, page 54)

100 g (3½ oz) filtered water, at room temperature

100 g (3½ oz) plain (all-purpose) spelt flour

455 g (1 lb) mixed sultanas (golden raisins), currants, muscatels and/or raisins

1 g (2 teaspoons) dried orange zest

355 g (12½ oz) freshly brewed Earl Grey tea

Like many Australians, we moved to London on a two-year working visa to have our first overseas adventure. Good thing we had the naivety of youth on our side because we knew absolutely no one in the UK, and also managed to spend all but $500 of the money we'd saved when we stopped off in Japan for three weeks to visit my brother, who was living there teaching. That's a story for another time.

It all worked out, though, as things usually do if you can find that slipstream of life and jump in with both feet. That's where I ran into Dale, who was managing an agency called Koala Nannies. I went in for an interview and came out with my first local friend — and a job. Five minutes into the conversation, I knew we'd be in each other's lives for a very long time, and that was even before he gave me his mum's traditional Welsh recipe for bara brith, handwritten on Welsh pony stationery. Yes, he's that guy. And 25 years on he's still one of my dearest friends, because if anything is going to seal that deal, it's cake and horses. And tea.

I've made this recipe with the tweak of sourdough starter in lieu of eggs, and Earl Grey tea with orange zest, because it's one of the first tea blends I did many years later when I started my first tea business. How brilliant is it when food provides so many threads to weave together across so many years and different experiences in life? Just lovely.

Bara brith — 'speckled bread' — is one of those uncomplicated comfort foods. Eat it fresh from the oven like cake, slice it and toast it to have with butter the next day, or freeze it so you have something on hand for morning tea when you haven't had time to bake.

You will need to start this the night before, to feed your sourdough starter and soak the dried fruit in the tea.

Remember to weigh all your ingredients, even the liquids.

DAY 1

Bring your sourdough starter to room temperature. Discard half the starter, to ensure a portion of the 'spent' starter that has exhausted its food source is removed, retaining the remaining starter for its microbial population.

Feed the remaining starter with 100 g (3½ oz) filtered room-temperature water and 100 g (3½ oz) flour (using the same type of flour you'll be using in your actual loaf). To do this, simply mix the flour and water into the starter and leave on the benchtop at room temperature overnight.

Meanwhile, soak the dried fruit and orange zest in the tea overnight.

90 g (3 oz) fed
sourdough starter
(from Day 1, opposite)

15 g (½ oz) ground
flaxseeds (linseeds)

400 g (14 oz) plain
(all-purpose) spelt flour

225 g (8 oz) rapadura
sugar

15 g (½ oz) baking
powder

7 g (1½ teaspoons)
Homemade Mixed
Spice (page 240)

5 g (1 teaspoon) salt

100 g (3½ oz) soy or
almond milk

35 g (1¼ oz) extra virgin
olive oil

The following morning, preheat your oven to 170ºC (325ºF). Line two loaf tins, measuring 20 cm (8 in) x 8 cm (3¼ in) x 6 cm (2½ in), with baking paper.

In a small bowl, mix the fed sourdough starter with the ground flaxseeds; the mixture will be quite thick. Leave for 10 minutes while you assemble the remaining ingredients, so the flaxseeds can absorb the liquid

In a large bowl, mix the flour, sugar, baking powder, mixed spice and salt together, ensuring any lumps of flour or sugar are completely dispersed.

Mix the milk and olive oil into the thickened sourdough mixture, until well incorporated. Now stir this mixture through the soaked fruit and tea.

Finally, add the wet mixture to the dry ingredients and stir until all the dry ingredients have been completely worked into a lovely thick batter.

Immediately spoon the batter into the loaf tins, dividing it evenly. Bake for 1 hour, or until the loaves are nicely browned on top and spring back to your touch.

Remove from the oven and leave to sit in the tins for 10 minutes before turning out onto a wire rack to cool. While they're still warm, I like to brush the top of the loaves with a little marmalade.

Time for tea.

Stored in an airtight container, the bara brith will keep for up to a week.

Sourdough Bara Brith (page 68), with my Barossa breakfast tea, and the neighbour's cows over the hill.

Plaited Sourdough Spiced Buns

Makes 8 buns

DAY 1

Sourdough starter
(see Language of
Sourdough, page 54)

100 g (3½ oz) plain
(all-purpose)
unbleached white
wheat flour

100 g (3½ oz) filtered
water, at room
temperature

DAY 2

150 g (5½ oz) fed
sourdough starter
(from Day 1, above)

180 g (6 oz) water

60 g (2 oz) extra virgin
olive oil, plus extra for
brushing the buns

50 g (1¾ oz) rapadura
sugar

10 g (⅓ oz) Homemade
Mixed Spice (page 240)

450 g (1 lb) unbleached
plain (all-purpose)
white spelt flour

5 g (1 teaspoon) salt

maple syrup or
marmalade, for glazing

This recipe is actually my hot cross bun recipe that I started making for Easter a few years ago. The thing is, I didn't want to stop making them once Easter was over because they had quickly become a lovely ritual with a pot of tea, filling the house with such an evocative smell of warm spices and baking bread that I felt like a character in an English novel. So the buns stayed, without their crosses and fruit, and plaited instead of rolled into little rounds.

I make these buns every Thursday to put in the fridge overnight and bake fresh on a Friday morning. The leftover buns get refreshed in an air-fryer or sandwich press on Saturday morning, when a couple of girlfriends and I get together to debrief after our week and drink a lot of tea.

If you don't want to bother with the four-strand plait, you can easily roll these into more traditional bun shapes. There's something quite meditative about plaiting the buns, though — it takes just long enough and requires just the right amount of your attention to quiet that little voice blabbing on about all the other things on your to-do list! I really love making them. And if you remember to keep taking the next strand of dough from the right-hand side of each bun, and always threading over and under, it becomes second nature in no time.

If you'd like to run with my timeline, I feed my starter on a Wednesday night before I go to bed, mix the bun dough using my electric mixer and a dough hook on Thursday morning, plait the buns and put them in the fridge on a tray Thursday afternoon, pull them out of the fridge first thing Friday morning to come up to room temperature while the oven is heating up, and we're eating warm buns with tea by 10 am Friday. It sets such a lovely rhythm to the week — and you've already fed your starter ready for baking bread on the weekend, too.

Remember to weigh all your ingredients, even the liquids.

DAY 1

Take your sourdough starter from the fridge and bring to room temperature. Discard half the starter, to ensure a portion of the 'spent' starter is removed. Feed your starter by mixing the flour and water into the starter and leave on the benchtop at room temperature overnight.

DAY 2

The next day, add the fed sourdough starter, water, olive oil, sugar and mixed spice to a large bowl sitting on a set of digital scales. (I use my Kitchen Aid for the dough making, but it can be done by hand, too.)

Add the flour and salt. Using the dough hook of your mixer, or by hand, knead the dough for 3–8 minutes, until smooth and elastic. If you're using a dough hook, you'll hear a change in the dough when the gluten activation has happened; it 'slaps' the bowl. Truly!

Cover the bowl with plastic wrap or a silicone cover. Leave at room temperature for 6–8 hours, or until the dough has nearly doubled in volume.

Cut the doubled dough into eight equal pieces and roll into balls.

Roll one of the balls into a sausage, then cut the sausage into four equal lengths.

Roll each of those pieces into a sausage, so you end up with four sausages about 15 cm (6 in) long and 1 cm (½ in) in diameter. Line them up in a row and pinch one end of the four sausages together so you can plait the whole thing into a bun without it coming apart. Taking the right-hand strip each time and threading it once over and under, plait the four strands together, then tuck the ends under to complete the bun.

Repeat with the remaining seven dough balls, to make eight buns.

Place the buns appropriately 1.5 cm (⅝ in) apart on a baking tray lined with baking paper. Drizzle a little olive oil into your hands and gently rub over the top and sides of each bun.

Cover the tray with plastic wrap (not too tightly; you don't want to squash the buns) and leave in the fridge overnight to prove.

DAY 3

Next morning, take the buns out of the fridge to come to room temperature while you heat your oven to 200°C (400°F).

When the oven is up to temperature, boil your kettle with at least 500 ml (17 fl oz) water. This is to add steam to your oven while the buns are baking. You'll also need an ovenproof dish to pour the water into; I use a bread tin on the shelf below the buns.

Place the tray of buns in the oven. Immediately add the boiled water to the pan you have placed underneath the buns. This will release lots of steam, which is what you want — so close the oven door quickly so the steam doesn't escape.

Bake for 25–30 minutes, watching the buns for that lovely deep golden colour. When you can feel they spring back to your touch, remove from the oven.

While still hot, brush maple syrup or marmalade over the top of each bun.

The buns will keep in an airtight container for up to 4 days. I like to warm them using a sandwich press or air-fryer if we're eating them any time after the day they were baked.

Sourdough Bagels

Makes 8 bagels

DAY 1

Sourdough starter (see
Language of Sourdough,
page 54)

200 g (7 oz) plain
(all-purpose)
unbleached white
spelt flour

200 g (7 oz) filtered
water, at room
temperature

DAY 2

150 g (5½ oz) filtered
water, at room
temperature

400 g (14 oz) fed
sourdough starter
(from Day 1, above)

40 g (1¼ oz) extra
virgin olive oil,
plus extra for oiling
the bagels

25 g (1 oz) rapadura
sugar, plus an extra
handful for the
boiling water

15 g (½ oz) salt

550 g (1 lb 4 oz)
plain (all-purpose)
unbleached white
spelt flour

sesame seeds,
poppy seeds or
rapadura sugar,
to coat

In many ways, making sourdough bagels is easier than making sourdough bread. I almost think of these bagels as the foolproof version of sourdough, as they can be slotted in just about anywhere you would enjoy a slice of bread.

This is another helpful recipe when you're making your own sourdough, because it's another great way to have something to make use of the first feed that you might otherwise dispose of when you're building your starter up to make a loaf.

Bagels look like they would be complicated, but once you break the process down over a few days — like most of the sourdough recipes in this chapter — making them becomes doable weekly. Get them started on a Saturday morning, and you'll be enjoying freshly baked bagels for Sunday brunch.

These are boiled and baked, like traditional bagels, but with my 'poke-a-hole' method of shaping them — another foolproof part of this recipe — you don't need to be overly dexterous to shape a beautiful bagel.

I love these savoury bagels with sesame or poppy seeds on top. If you'd like a sweet version, try adding dried fruit and topping with rapadura sugar.

Remember to weigh all your ingredients, even the liquids.

DAY 1

Take your sourdough starter from the fridge and bring to room temperature. Discard half the starter, then mix the flour and water into the remaining starter and leave on the benchtop at room temperature overnight.

DAY 2

Place a large mixing bowl on your digital scales and tare. Pour the water into the bowl. Add the fed sourdough starter, olive oil, sugar and salt, stirring well. Add the flour and stir until completely combined, making sure there are no dry pockets of flour.

Knead on a clean bench for 3–4 minutes, until the dough becomes nice and springy. Place back in the bowl, cover and leave in a warm place to rise for 3–4 hours, until doubled in size.

Divide the dough into eight equal pieces, then roll each piece into a ball.

Using your thumb and index finger, pinch through the centre of a dough ball — and then, using both index fingers, create the centre of the bagel by rolling your fingers around each other. It may not be the daintiest option, but I find this method of shaping way easier than the traditional rolling and joining back together technique.

Once all the bagels are shaped, place them on a non-stick baking tray. Pour a little olive oil into your hands and gently rub across the top of each bagel. Cover with plastic wrap and place in the fridge overnight.

DAY 3

Take the bagels out of the fridge and preheat your oven to 200°C (400°F).

Bring a large pot of water to the boil with a small handful of rapadura sugar thrown in, to give a lovely gloss to the bagels when they are baking. Depending on the size of your pan, gently drop two, three or four bagels into the boiling water. Let the bagels boil on one side for 30–60 seconds until slightly puffed, then flip them over with a slotted spoon to boil on the other side for 30 seconds. Remove from the water and drain on a wire rack set over a baking tray.

While you boil the next lot of bagels, coat the just-boiled bagels in your choice of seeds — or rapadura sugar for a sweeter option. Spread the seeds or sugar evenly across a plate and then, one at a time, upend each bagel onto the seeds or sugar before flipping it back up to have the coating sitting on top.

Once you have boiled and coated each bagel, place them back on the wire rack set over the baking tray, then transfer to the oven and bake for 20 minutes.

Hot bagels are yours. Enjoy as you normally would, or try them with any of the brunch offerings in Chapter One. The bagels will keep in an airtight container for 3–5 days. Once they are past their day of baking, toast them before serving.

Sourdough Banana & Chamomile Muffins

Makes 10–12 muffins, depending on your tin size

90 g (3 oz) sourdough starter, fed the night before with 50 g (1¾ oz) each flour and water (see Language of Sourdough, page 54)

15 g (½ oz) ground flaxseeds (linseeds)

350 g (12 oz) plain (all-purpose) unbleached white spelt flour

180 g (6 oz) rapadura sugar

5 g (2 teaspoons) ground cinnamon

5 g (1 teaspoon) salt

3 g (¾ teaspoon) bicarbonate of soda (baking soda)

1 g (¼ teaspoon) baking powder

150 g (5½ oz) fresh strong-brewed chamomile tea, cooled

150 g (5½ oz) soy or almond milk

100 g (3½ oz) extra virgin olive oil

300 g (10½ oz) bananas, mashed

200 g (7 oz) walnuts

Muffins are an excellent place to start if you want to begin experimenting with using your sourdough starter in baking, because they are so forgiving. This is another chance to play around with flaxseeds as a binding agent, too, and while I wouldn't recommend you sub in sourdough and flaxseeds for light, airy cakes such as a sponge, it absolutely works with anything on the more rustic end of the baking scale — which is where I place muffins.

It's also well worth experimenting with including tea in cooking. No need to mention again how much I love tea, but the beautiful hint of chamomile tea is just so lovely with the banana in these muffins. When you see liquids such as plain water or milk in any baking recipe, try replacing it with cooled tea.

And the last little trick I'll mention here is making your own muffin tin liners. Simply tear off 12–15 cm (4½–6 in) squares of baking paper and push them into your muffin tin with the base of a glass. Personally, I think they look cuter than store-bought muffin cases. The things you learn when you don't live close enough to just pop to the shops!

You'll need to begin this recipe by feeding your starter the night before with 50 g (1¾ oz) plain (all-purpose) unbleached white spelt flour and 50 g (1¾ oz) water. Remember to weigh all your ingredients, even the liquids.

Preheat your oven to 180°C (350°F). Line a 10-hole or 12-hole muffin tray with muffin cases or baking paper (see above).

In a medium bowl placed on a set of digital scales, weigh out the fed sourdough starter and ground flaxseeds, then mix together; the mixture will be quite thick. Leave for 10 minutes while you assemble the remaining ingredients.

In a large bowl (again set on your scales), weigh out the flour, sugar, cinnamon, salt, bicarbonate of soda and baking powder, then mix together.

Place the bowl containing the sourdough starter and flaxseed mixture back on the scales, and add the chamomile tea, milk, olive oil and mashed banana. Mix thoroughly, but don't worry about any lumpy bits of sourdough starter or banana — you just want them evenly distributed in the mix.

Add the wet ingredients to the dry and mix until combined. Add the walnuts and continue stirring to make sure all traces of dry ingredients are mixed in.

Spoon the batter into the muffin holes, filling each three-quarters full.

Bake for 30–35 minutes, or until the tops are nicely browned and spring back to your touch.

Leave in the tin for a few minutes before turning out onto a wire rack to cool. The muffins will keep in an airtight container for 3–5 days.

Sourdough Pasta Dough

*Makes about 275 g
(9¾ oz)*

120 g (4 oz) semolina
flour

5 g (1 teaspoon) salt

120 g (4 oz) sourdough
starter (unfed, at room
temperature; see
Language of Sourdough,
page 54)

30–50 g (1–1¾ oz) water

This is another great basic recipe to have — and yet more proof that once the sourdough bug bites, it really bites hard. Nothing escapes a fermented makeover once your brain is switched to sourdough, so it didn't take me long to try the idea of incorporating sourdough into pasta-making, because they both rate highly in our house.

If you make the pasta dough, wrap it and leave it in the fridge overnight, before rolling it out the next day, you'll be more inspired to add this into your weekly routine, rather than keep it for special occasions. It still feels incredibly special, though, and I will always make this pasta if we have friends coming over. That's another good reason to make the dough the day before, so when friends or family arrive for lunch, they get to share in the rolling and cutting — which we all know is the fun bit!

Kids especially love rolling pasta through a hand-cranked pasta machine, and then you can let them go wild with shaping it, because this dough recipe is pretty resilient. It can be made into hand-cut tagliatelle, cavatelli (page 122), filled with Almond Ricotta (page 227) and turned into ravioli, or used to make something more substantial like a rotolo (page 130). Don't tell the traditionalists, but I've also used this dough in lieu of egg noodles in soup.

You won't necessarily need to feed your starter the night before for this recipe, as it doesn't rely on the starter for any rising action — more for flavour than anything else. Just be sure you have about 150 g (5½ oz) of starter in the fridge. If not, remove the starter from the fridge and feed it with 100 g (3½ oz) water and 100 g (3½ oz) flour the night before.

Remember to weigh all your ingredients, even the water.

In a food processor, briefly mix the semolina and salt.

Mix the sourdough starter and water together in a small jug. With the food processor running, pour the mixture in a little at a time, until the dough comes together.

Turn out onto a clean bench and knead for 5–10 minutes, until the dough is smooth and no longer sticky. If you need a little extra semolina here, be careful not to add too much, or you will very quickly make the pasta too dry. (I always knead my pasta dough on a marble cutting board, so I don't need to add any extra flour to stop it sticking.)

Wrap in plastic wrap and rest the dough for 20 minutes. Alternatively, you can leave the dough in the fridge to use the next day. You will need to take it out of the fridge and let it come up to room temperature, before kneading it by hand for 5–10 minutes; you can then run it through a pasta machine or roll it out by hand, using a rolling pin.

Sourdough Black Tea Kvass

*Makes about 2 litres
(70 fl oz)*

2 litres (70 fl oz) freshly brewed Earl Grey tea, cooled to room temperature

300 g (10½ oz) sourdough crusts, toasted (for extra flavour) and roughly chopped into big bits

130 g (4½ oz) rapadura sugar

30 g (1 oz) blackstrap molasses

25 g (1 oz) sourdough starter (unfed, at room temperature; see Language of Sourdough, page 54)

Kvass is a traditional eastern European fermented drink and one of those things I always thought sounded really good for you in a particularly exotic way. I had only ever tried kvass made with beetroot juice, but of course there's never only one way to do things, especially when it comes to ferments, so the idea of a tea kvass piqued my interest in a whole new way.

Once I'd made this a few times, I was brave (or silly) enough to make it for a friend who is a well-known winemaker here in the Barossa. Although the idea of taking a homemade alcohol-free beverage to someone who practises the complex art of oenology might seem like setting myself up for harsh critiquing, he absolutely loved it.

I felt so excited when he swirled the kvass, checked the colour against the light, put his nose all the way into the glass and did that especially audible final tasting to see how it fared on his palate; it was a proper, grown-up appreciation of the kvass, which is anything but a kid's drink. I haven't had alcohol for years, but I really love how this kvass fills the space where a dark stout might sit on a cold winter's night.

Put all the ingredients in a very clean, dry 3 litre (105 fl oz) glass jar and stir. Cover the open top of the jar with muslin (cheesecloth) or a clean tea towel to keep bugs out, but still allow the mixture to breathe.

Leave the kvass on the kitchen bench for 2 days at room temperature. Stir each day, but only to move the sourdough crusts around a bit — don't over-agitate the mixture.

Once the kvass starts to show fizziness, it's ready to drink, but will contain some alcohol. If you're happy with this, you can either strain the solids out through a piece of muslin — or leave some bread sediment in the bottom, in the style of a cloudy stout.

Taste it after 24 hours. If it's to your liking, put a lid on the jar and store it in the fridge. Remember to 'burp' the bottle or jar by briefly taking the lid off every few days while it's in the fridge, to release built-up gas — otherwise it can explode!

We usually drink this amount across a weekend. The kvass will last in the fridge for at least a week, but will continue to change as it ages and become slightly more acidic.

Sourdough Bread & Quince Jelly Ice Cream

Serves 6–8

190 g (6½ oz) cashews

400 g (14 oz) coconut cream (don't try to use coconut milk here)

80 g (2¾ oz) maple syrup

40 g (1½ oz) rapadura sugar

8 g (2 teaspoons) vanilla bean paste

20 g (¾ oz) coconut oil, solid, not melted

INCLUSIONS

150 g (5½ oz) Sourdough Bread (page 58), cut into 1 cm (½ in) cubes

50 g (1¾ oz) sesame seeds

100 g (3½ oz) quince jelly, or your choice of jam

I know how annoying it is to get excited about an ice cream recipe — only to read that you need an ice cream machine to make it, so I'm just going to say it right up front: ice cream machines really do create the best ice cream, and I've only ever been disappointed trying to make an ice cream without one. Sorry to burst that bubble, but honesty is best when it comes to something as serious as homemade ice cream!

After making yet another batch of hard, ice-crystal-laden ice cream lacking that prized creamy mouthfeel, I remember heading to the local electrical store prepared to get the best ice cream machine ever, just so I didn't waste another lot of beautiful ingredients, not to mention time and effort. Our local electrical store is neither large nor particularly well stocked, but I still managed to get a perfectly good machine for a surprisingly reasonable price, and it absolutely does the job — cooling and churning at the same time is very hard to replicate by hand.

You're going to love this ice cream. This is my favourite ice cream base, and once it's been churned, you can add all kinds of extras to it.

I have used all different kinds of jam in lieu of the quince jelly in this recipe, but if you're a quince devotee, this will be your new favourite thing. With the almost honeycomb crunch of the toasted sourdough, and the umami of the toasted sesame seeds, it's fancy in a very rustic way. Farmhouse fancy.

You'll need to begin this recipe the day before, soaking the cashews overnight. I make this in a 20 cm (8 in) loaf tin, so the ice cream can either be scooped out, or cut into slices like an ice cream terrine.

Remember to measure everything in grams, even the liquids.

Soak the cashews overnight in water.

Next day, before you make your ice cream base, preheat your oven to 150°C (300°F), to toast the sourdough. Place the sourdough cubes in a single layer on a flat baking tray and bake for 10–15 minutes, until nicely coloured. Allow to cool and become extra crispy.

To toast the sesame seeds, simply add to a dry frying pan and cook over medium heat for a minute or two, until golden and super fragrant. Keep a vigilant watch as they cook, because sesame seeds can burn very quickly. Once toasted, set aside to cool.

To make the ice cream, drain the cashews and place in a high-speed blender. Add the coconut cream, maple syrup, sugar and vanilla paste and blitz until very smooth. Add the coconut oil and briefly blitz again to emulsify the mixture, without heating the oil too much and risk the mixture splitting.

Pour the mixture into your ice cream machine and follow the manufacturer's churning instructions.

Line a 20 cm (8 in) x 8 cm (3¼ in) x 6 cm (2½ in) loaf tin with baking paper, leaving enough paper overhanging to wrap right over the top of the ice cream once it's layered in the tin.

Place half the ice cream in the tin and roughly even it out. Top with randomly spaced spoonfuls of quince jelly. Gently push the sourdough cubes into the jelly and ice cream, then sprinkle with half the sesame seeds. Add the remaining ice cream and sprinkle with the remaining sesame seeds.

Wrap the baking paper over to completely cover the top. Place in the freezer to set for at least 3 hours; it will keep frozen for up to a month.

This is a seriously dense ice cream — no whipped air here! — so take it out of the freezer at least 15 minutes before serving. Either scoop or slice — your choice.

HEARTY SALADS

As soon as you have a vegie garden, you automatically have new salad combinations at your fingertips, with seasonal greens in ready supply. You'll also be able to access the complete growing cycle of plants — the seeds, flowers, tendrils and pollen that you just won't find in a supermarket. We often let the vegie garden plan the menu, simply by picking what's right in front of us.

Anyone plant-based or wanting to eat more plants will tell you that when it comes to salad as the real deal, a lettuce and cucumber side salad is not going to cut it. So, the salads in this chapter will happily sit where any main meal might; they're the satisfying star of the show rather than an afterthought. Even my dad, who is very hard to please when it comes to salad, will always have a quiet second helping of the salad options when he comes to our place for a meal.

Snow Pea, Tofu, Nashi, Green Tea & Arame Salad

20 g (¾ oz) green tea leaves

25 g (1 oz) dried arame seaweed (available from health food stores)

300 g (10½ oz) firm Homemade Tofu (page 236)

250 g (9 oz) snow peas (mange tout) and tendrils, if available

300 g (10½ oz) cucumber

1 nashi pear (200 g/7 oz)

50 g (1¾ oz) snow pea (mange tout) sprouts

30 g (1 oz) Sprouted Almonds (page 243)

8 g (2 teaspoons) Green Gomasio (page 234)

20 ml (½ fl oz) sesame oil

15 ml (½ fl oz) mirin

5 g (1 teaspoon) salt

Eating green tea leaves is not something I had ever considered before my most recent trip to Japan — even though I use tea in cooking all the time. My brother and I went to the most beautiful tea ceremony in Tokyo where, along with different kinds of green tea and matcha, a perfectly imperfect, handmade pottery plate was delivered with a small scoop of the green tea leaves used to brew our previous pot of tea, with a set of chopsticks on the side. The presentation was so stunning I sat for a moment just looking at the plate, until the tea master gently said to me, 'You can eat them.' Of course! Why didn't I think of this before?

I came home and made a salad purely so I could eat tea leaves again, adding other elements of inspiration from our trip: arame seaweed (which isn't strong in 'fishy' flavour, but has the most delicious springy texture), nashi pear, gomasio and sesame. To give it a farmy twist, I included cucumber, snow peas and tendrils from our garden, along with my latest Japanese-inspired obsession — homemade tofu.

I definitely don't want you to deny yourself this salad based on making your own tofu, so go ahead and enjoy it with a good store-bought tofu — but I would love you to have a go at making tofu, as much for the ritual as for the taste.

Brew yourself a pot of green tea using the green tea leaves and enjoy sipping on the liquid while the spent tea leaves cool, ready to add to the salad.

Rinse the arame seaweed thoroughly. Place in a medium saucepan with plenty of water, as it will expand up to four times in volume as it rehydrates. Bring to the boil over high heat, then reduce the heat and simmer for 15 minutes, or until tender. Drain the seaweed and allow to cool while you prepare the remaining salad ingredients.

Cut the tofu into 2 cm (¾ in) cubes and halve the snow peas length ways. Slice the cucumber into 1 cm (½ in) thick rounds, then into half-moons. Thinly slice the pear, after removing the core.

Place all the ingredients, except the tofu (so it doesn't break up too much), in a large serving bowl. Stir well to ensure the mirin and sesame oil are evenly distributed throughout the salad.

Add the tofu and give a final, gentle stir-through. Garnish with snow pea tendrils, if you have some, and serve immediately.

Watermelon, Olive, Mint & Almond Ricotta Salad

Serves 2–4

GLUTEN FREE

650 g (1 lb 7 oz) watermelon, cut into wedges, rind removed

70 g (2½ oz) kalamata olives, pitted and torn in half

100 g (3½ oz) Almond Ricotta (page 227)

a small handful of mint leaves

20 ml (½ fl oz) extra virgin olive oil

On really hot days, this salad is like a salve. I know watermelon salads are typically made with feta, but there's something about the combination of sweet watermelon, salty olives and the creaminess of the almond ricotta that is just so delicious.

I always notice the olive oil in this salad, so I'd suggest getting your hands on the 'grassiest' olive oil you can for this, because when there's so few ingredients, you want to use the freshest and most flavourful of each.

Which brings me to mint. I know I harp on about growing herbs, but even the smallest inner-city balcony can host a pot of mint — which is so amazing picked fresh, and so disappointing if pulled all limp from a plastic supermarket sleeve. This salad definitely makes a case for having homegrown mint on hand.

Place the watermelon wedges on a serving platter. Top with the olives and dollops of ricotta. Scatter the mint leaves across the salad and drizzle with the olive oil. Season with salt to taste.

Serve immediately, with sourdough slices to mop up the juices.

Glasshouse Tomato Sourdough Panzanella

Serves 2–4

300 g (10½ oz)
day-old Sourdough
Bread (page 58)

350 g (12 oz) mixed
tomatoes, such as roma
(plum), cherry, oxheart
and mortgage lifter

50 g (1¾ oz) kalamata
olives, pitted

30 g (1 oz) capers

20 g (¾ oz) basil leaves

5 g (3 teaspoons)
marjoram leaves

60 ml (2 fl oz) balsamic
vinegar

50 ml (1¾ fl oz) extra
virgin olive oil

My dad was a master tomato grower when we were kids. He took tomato growing very seriously, mostly because he is one of the fussiest people I know when it comes to tomatoes — he'd rather go without than compromise on flavour. My brother inherited the same tomato fixation. When we lived together as adults in North Melbourne many years later, we dedicated the only space in the tiny yard of our rented terrace house to tomato growing. He even grew tomatoes on his apartment balcony in Bangkok, and we made a vegie garden in the parking lot at Eat Me, trying in vain to bring the Mediterranean flavour of our hot, dry, sun-drenched South Australian childhood to the tropical, humid climate of Thailand. Tomatoes hold a disproportionately important place in our family is what I'm getting at, so when we finally built the glasshouse on our hill in the Barossa, the first thing that went in were tomatoes.

We planted as many different kinds of tomatoes as we could in that debut season, so we could see what would work best. Turns out they all liked it here and so each year we now end up with an array of tomatoes in different colours and sizes — all with that unmistakable fragrance that envelops you when you brush past their leaves hunting for ripe fruit. I love sharing them with Mum and Dad, especially now they no longer have a vegie garden. Dad doesn't say much when I hand over a paper bag of still-warm fruit. He just brings a tomato to his nose and gives a bit of a nod, but I know the master's cycle has been successfully completed!

Panzanella is one of the best ways I know to really let good tomatoes shine. It's also one of my favourite uses for sourdough that has gone past the point of sandwiches and into toast territory. The smell of ripe tomatoes and fragrant herbs is the signature scent of summer for me.

Tear the bread into 2–3 cm (¾–1¼ in) pieces and toss into a large bowl. Slice the tomatoes and add to the bowl, then stir through to release some of the tomato juices for the bread to soak up.

Add the olives, capers, basil and marjoram and stir through. Drizzle with the vinegar and olive oil. Season to taste with salt and black pepper and stir through again to ensure the balsamic and olive oil have been taken up by the bread.

Allow to sit for a few minutes before serving, so the flavours can meld.

Seedy Brussels Sprouts Slaw

Serves 2–4

GLUTEN FREE

50 g (1¾ oz) pepitas
(pumpkin seeds)

50 g (1¾ oz) sunflower
seeds

300 g (10½ oz) brussels
sprouts

1 apple (100 g/3½ oz)

1 large fennel bulb
(250 g/9 oz), with fronds
attached

100 g (3½ oz) carrots,
scrubbed (purple
carrots look beautiful,
if available)

30 g (1 oz) dill

100 ml (3½ fl oz)
coconut cream

30 ml (1 fl oz) Apple
Cider Vinegar (page 178)

100 g (3½ oz) hemp
seeds

We have tried growing brussels sprouts many times — but we always end up with slightly stunted, odd-shaped, often earwig-nibbled little globes instead of plump, glossy brussels sprouts. And what do you do with those? Coleslaw, that's what. When you consider that brussels sprouts are really just tiny cabbages, it's an easy next step to sub them into your favourite coleslaw recipe in lieu of traditional cabbage. And shredding them helps manoeuvre around any blemishes in homegrown brussels sprouts, without completely discarding them. I actually prefer them to a larger cabbage in coleslaw now. They're softer somehow, but still offer a lovely punch of flavour when used raw.

I'm a big fan of brussels sprouts, regardless of how they're prepared, but if they're not near the top of your favourites list, trying them raw and finely shaved in a salad like this might be a great place to change that relationship — presuming we even have a relationship with brussels sprouts? Gawd, let's just eat coleslaw...

Toast the pepitas and sunflower seeds in a dry frying pan over high heat for a minute or two, until they start to brown and smell beautifully fragrant. Remove from the heat and leave to cool.

Very finely slice the brussels sprouts, apple and fennel; I use my food processor for this, then swap the blade to a grater for the carrots — but you could also use a mandoline to grate the carrots. Toss the brussels sprouts, apple, fennel and grated carrot together in a serving bowl, with the fennel fronds and dill.

In a smaller bowl, whisk together the coconut cream and vinegar. Season with salt to taste.

Pour the dressing over the salad, stirring it through thoroughly to coat everything really well. Add the toasted seeds and hemp seeds. Mix again and adjust the seasoning if necessary.

Serve immediately, while the slaw is still fresh and full of crunchy vitality.

Asparagus, Potato & Broad Bean Salad

Serves 2–4

GLUTEN FREE

500 g (1 lb 2 oz) potatoes

320 g (11 oz) asparagus

300 g (10½ oz) broad beans

250 g (9 oz) cooked chickpeas, or drained tinned chickpeas

30 g (1 oz) capers

30 g (1 oz) dill, chopped

50 ml (1¾ fl oz) extra virgin olive oil

30 ml (1 fl oz) lemon juice

8 g (2 teaspoons) Green Gomasio (page 234)

When we were filming the first television season of *All The Things*, it happened to be asparagus season. Had we been relying on what meagre offerings I persist in tending from my own asparagus crowns, I certainly wouldn't have based an episode around it, but my friend Richard literally has a paddock of wild asparagus that comes up each spring — and that is definitely worth getting the cameras out for! I'd never seen asparagus growing wild before. It was such an amazing thing to walk through a field of it, picking spears as we went.

Wild asparagus is thinner than the cultivated variant, and the tips far less pronounced, but it is so full of flavour I ate every second spear raw as we harvested them. Of course you don't need to find wild asparagus for this salad, but asparagus still varies wildly in quality depending on where you buy it. Our local farmers' market is always my first port of call, because that's the closest and freshest I'll get to homegrown. You will absolutely notice the comparison to fresh produce that has been shipped to supermarkets, especially with something like asparagus that has such a short season.

Our homegrown potatoes and broad beans were ready in the garden when we went foraging for asparagus at Richard's place, and they make for earthy, delicious companions in this salad, which has all the satisfying aspects of a traditional potato salad, but with the seasonal touches of spring. I love eating this salad, but it's fair to say I love collecting the ingredients even more if it involves a call from Richard.

Scrub the potatoes and cut into quarters. Place in a large saucepan, cover with cold water and bring to the boil. Cook for 8–10 minutes, or until tender. Drain and set aside to cool.

Cut the asparagus into 5 cm (2 inch) lengths and blanch in a large saucepan of boiling water for no more than 2–3 minutes. Drain and set aside to cool.

Snap the broad bean pods apart down their seams and extract the beans. Blanch the beans in a saucepan of boiling water and for 3–5 minutes, or until tender. (I don't bother about double-peeling broad beans if I've just picked them from the garden and they're on the smaller side, but if you think there's any toughness in the skins of your broad beans, definitely take them off, to reveal that amazing verdant green bean underneath.)

Assemble the salad on a large platter, layering the potatoes on the bottom, followed by the asparagus. Layer the broad beans and chickpeas across the asparagus, then scatter the capers and dill over the top.

Pour the lemon juice and olive oil over the layered ingredients. Sprinkle the gomasio over the whole salad to season, then serve.

Shaved Fennel with Blood Orange, Radish, Mint & Chickpeas

Serves 2–4

GLUTEN FREE

2 g (1 teaspoon) fennel seeds

2 blood oranges (250 g/9 oz)

1 large fennel bulb (120 g/4 oz), shaved, fronds reserved

2 small radishes (20 g/¾ oz), shaved

250 g (9 oz) cooked chickpeas, or drained tinned chickpeas

a small handful of mint leaves

10 g (1½ tablespoons) roughly chopped flat-leaf parsley

5 g (3 teaspoons) chopped marjoram leaves

50 ml (1¾ fl oz) extra virgin olive oil

Here's another salad that came about in our farmhouse and made its way onto the restaurant menu in Bangkok. One of the things I love about having fennel in the garden is that I have access to the full cycle of the plant — fronds, bulbs, flowers, pollen and seeds. Our fennel is rotating through its stages year round, so there's always a reason to include it in my cooking. I also love picking the stalks of pollen-laden flowers to have in a vase, for their rustic beauty alone.

This recipe, though, is all about the bulbs when they are in season, and I really think a mandoline is called for to really get the best result, giving you wafer-thin cross-section slices of raw fennel that allow the juice from the orange to almost marinate them as the salad is coming together. Blood oranges are perfectly timed to coincide with fennel season, but navel or valencia oranges will also be delicious in this dish.

I cook most of my pulses in my pressure cooker these days, by soaking them overnight and then cooking for 20 minutes the next day. I love freshly cooked chickpeas, but by no means are they a deal-breaker in this salad, so I've included the equivalent weight from a 400 g (14 oz) tin of chickpeas to make this easy to put together at the last minute.

Toast the fennel seeds in a dry frying pan over high heat for a minute or two, until they start to brown and smell beautifully fragrant. Remove from the heat and leave to cool.

Zest the oranges and set the zest aside for the dressing. Cut the oranges into segments. To do this, hold the oranges over a bowl to catch any juice, then cut the citrus into segments by removing the skin and cutting from the outside in towards the centre, running your knife along the inside line of membrane of each segment. This will allow you to remove a wedge of membrane-free orange and is also known as 'supreming'. Continue working your way around the orange segments, retaining the juices for the dressing.

In a large bowl, gently toss together the orange segments, shaved fennel, radish and chickpeas. Add the mint, parsley, marjoram and reserved fennel fronds.

Whisk together the olive oil, orange zest and reserved orange juice. Season with salt to taste.

Drizzle the dressing over the salad, sprinkle with the toasted fennel seeds and serve immediately.

Purple Carrot, Fig & Pearl Barley Salad

Serves 2–4

400 g (14 oz) purple carrots, raw or roasted

100 ml (3½ fl oz) extra virgin olive oil

250 g (9 oz) pearl barley

50–80 g (1¾–2¾ oz) radicchio leaves

250 g (9 oz) fresh figs, halved down the middle

200 g (7 oz) purple grapes, halved lengthways

2 teaspoons thyme leaves

3 teaspoons roughly chopped parsley

BALSAMIC ZA'ATAR DRESSING

40 ml (1¼ fl oz) extra virgin olive oil

20 ml (½ fl oz) balsamic vinegar

8 g (2½ teaspoons) za'atar spice mix

5 g (1 teaspoon) salt

I would happily put fresh figs in everything when they're in season. Years ago, in Bangkok, I was helping out with the menu at Eat Me and the most amazing fresh figs were coming in from one of our Australian suppliers. It was only when my brother suggested we didn't need to have a 'Fig Festival' that I realised how many dishes, both sweet and savoury, I'd added them to. Oops. I might have a fig blindspot, it seems — but when our five fig trees are all offering up their jammy bounty at once, I'm grateful for my fig-based single-mindedness. After living in Sydney and happily paying $3 a fig just to get my fix, having them in abundance is something that never gets old for me. There's the unmistakable taste and texture of a perfectly ripe fig, but the colour palette is also something I'm in awe of every time I split one open. So. Beautiful.

This salad is as much about the visuals of all those deep purple tones coming together as it is about how deliciously the individual flavours hold hands. It might also be a chance to remember just how good pearl barley is, too — such a satisfying, spongy little grain, and often forgotten.

I keep roasted carrots from my weekly roast, and use them at room temperature in this salad. If you'd like a warm version of this salad, roast the carrots as instructed below, and use the pearl barley warm, too.

If you haven't included carrots in your weekly roast, preheat your oven to 200°C (400°F). Scrub the carrots, rather than peel them, and cut in half lengthways. Place in a baking dish and drizzle with the olive oil. Season with salt and black pepper, cover with foil and bake for 30 minutes. Remove the foil, give the carrots a bit of a stir-through to coat with olive oil from the bottom of the pan, then roast, uncovered, for a further 30 minutes, or until tender.

Cook the pearl barley following the packet instructions, then drain. Either leave to cool, or use warm.

On a serving platter, layer the pearl barley, radicchio and roasted carrots. Add the fig halves, grapes and herbs.

Whisk the dressing ingredients together, then drizzle over the salad and serve immediately.

Shaved Broccoli, Rocket, Grapefruit & Avocado Salad

Serves 2–4

GLUTEN FREE

400 g (14 oz) broccoli

2 small radishes (20 g/¾ oz)

1 ruby grapefruit (200 g/7 oz)

1 avocado (150 g/ 5½ oz), sliced

50–70 g (1¾–2½ oz) rocket (arugula) leaves (and flowers, if possible)

50 g (1¾ oz) dried pear, cut into 1 cm (½ in) cubes

50 ml (1¾ fl oz) extra virgin olive oil

10 g (2 teaspoons) Green Gomasio (page 234)

If there's one thing that never fails in our winter garden, it's broccoli — and even though we plant more seeds each year, we still never seem to have enough. When the good broccoli times are rolling, we eat like broccoli kings and pretty much have broccoli every day, so it was inevitable that I'd try it in its raw state. What a delicious revelation. Finely shaved broccoli paired with the creaminess of avocado and a little bitter edge from the grapefruit combine to make a salad that I'll happily eat on its own. It's also really gorgeous with grilled tofu tossed through, or piled onto a burger, or into a bagel. Think of it as a spin on coleslaw and you'll come up with lots of ways to include raw broccoli on your plate. I think it looks really beautiful, too, because it keeps that vibrant just-picked green colour that makes you feel healthier just looking at it.

Finely shave the broccoli and radishes using a mandoline or very sharp knife. Place in a large serving bowl.

Holding the grapefruit over a bowl to catch any juice, cut the citrus into segments by removing the skin and cutting from the outside in towards the centre, running your knife along the inside line of membrane of each segment. This will allow you to remove a wedge of membrane-free grapefruit, and is also known as 'supreming'. Continue working your way around the grapefruit segments, retaining the juices for the dressing.

Add the grapefruit segments to the salad, along with the avocado, rocket and pear, and gently toss together.

In a small bowl, whisk the grapefruit juice and olive oil to emulsify. Pour the dressing over the salad ingredients and stir through thoroughly, to ensure an even coating.

Sprinkle with the gomasio and serve immediately.

Cauliflower Salad with Capers, Pomegranate, Dill & Pickled Fennel Flowers

Serves 2–4

GLUTEN FREE

50 g (1¼ oz) pepitas (pumpkin seeds)

1 pomegranate (90 g/3 oz)

50–70 g (1¾–2½ oz) rocket (arugula) leaves (and flowers, if possible)

700 g (1 lb 9 oz) cauliflower, roasted (see tip, page 129)

180 g (6 oz) Almond Ricotta (page 227)

15 g (½ oz) Pickled Fennel Flowers (page 170)

30 g (1 oz) capers

10 g (⅓ oz) dill fronds

50 ml (1¾ fl oz) extra virgin olive oil

We usually have great success growing cauliflower in our garden, but fail to stagger the planting and end up eating it in a marathon of recipes. One of my favourite reasons to include cauliflower in salads or pasta is because it grabs hold of flavour in its cumulus-cloud hands, yet still manages to retain a subtle sense of crunch without becoming soggy. I also love the golden colour roasted cauliflower takes on.

I first made this salad when some girlfriends came for lunch and, in typical fashion, arrived bearing a bounty of produce from their gardens. Serendipity was on our side. The tray of roasted cauliflower I had on hand from my weekly roast happily joined forces with homegrown pomegranates from one friend, a bunch of fresh dill from another, and the most beautiful olive oil that had just been bottled that week.

I had planned to serve Pickled Fennel Flowers (page 170) as a pre-lunch nibble with sourdough, but we were all talking too much and I forgot about them until I put the salad down — so I added them at the table instead. They're not essential, and don't make or break this dish, but gosh they were good with the cauliflower and pomegranate.

Toast the pepitas in a dry frying pan over high heat for a minute or two, until they start to brown and smell beautifully fragrant. Remove from the heat and set aside to cool.

Split the pomegranate open and separate the seeds (arils) from the pith. Do this over a bowl, to catch any juices that might be squeezed out while handling the pomegranate.

On a large serving platter, layer the rocket leaves and roasted cauliflower pieces.

Top with spoonfuls of the almond ricotta and scatter the pomegranate seeds, pickled fennel flowers, capers and toasted pepitas across the salad.

Finish with the dill fronds and rocket flowers, if you have them. Finally, dress with the olive oil and any retained pomegranate juices.

Season with salt to taste, then serve.

Roasted Pear & Parsnip Salad

Serves 2–4

GLUTEN FREE

1 kg (2 lb 4 oz) parsnips

100 ml (3½ fl oz) extra virgin olive oil

450 g (1 lb) brown pears, such as beurre bosc

5 g (3 teaspoons) thyme leaves

200 g (7 oz) macadamia nuts

3 g (1 teaspoon) coriander seeds

10 g (⅓ oz) coriander (cilantro) leaves

10 g (⅓ oz) roughly chopped flat-leaf parsley

10 g (⅓ oz) Red Lentil Sprouts (page 242)

edible flowers, to garnish (optional)

FOR THE DRESSING

50 ml (1¾ fl oz) extra virgin olive oil

20 ml (½ fl oz) verjuice

When we lived in London, we quickly adopted the English tradition of Sunday lunch at a pub — which, unlike many Australian pubs, is more like going to a very relaxed, very local restaurant that just happens to include a bar. The kind of place that has window boxes filled with geraniums and people playing chess.

Our local was The Westbourne in Notting Hill. We loved having late lunch there with friends on any given Sunday because the food was so reliably good. I loved their roast parsnip and pear salad so much that I ordered it every week until they changed the menu.

What follows isn't the exact same salad, but it's the best rendition my food brain has archived from my memory of its flavours and textures. I've added some optional homegrown touches with the nasturtiums and lentil sprouts.

I love how roasting vegetables deepens their flavour, but I never knew the same would be the case for pears. Roasted brown pears are just so good — especially with roasted parsnip! Keep a few roasted pears back for your breakfast the next day if you can. They're delicious alongside the Almond Ricotta with Roasted Almonds, Lavender & Coconut syrup recipe on page 41.

Preheat your oven to 200°C (400°F).

Scrub the parsnips, rather than peel them, then cut in half lengthways. Place in a baking dish and drizzle with the olive oil. Season with salt and black pepper, cover with foil and bake for 30 minutes. Remove the foil, then give the parsnips a bit of a stir to coat them with the olive oil from the bottom of the pan. Roast, uncovered, for a further 15 minutes, or until tender.

Quarter the pears and remove their core and seeds. Open the oven door and carefully add the pears and thyme to the parsnip baking dish, spooning some of the roasting oil across the pears. Roast for a further 15 minutes, or until the parsnip and pears are tender and golden brown along their edges.

With 5–8 minutes of roasting time left, sneak in the macadamias to toast on a separate baking tray. No need to add anything to the macadamias while they're roasting — just keep an eye on them so they don't burn. Cool, then roughly chop.

Once tender, remove the pears and parsnip from the oven, along with the roasted macadamias, and allow to cool to room temperature.

In a dry frying pan over high heat, toast the coriander seeds. After about 2–3 minutes, they will start to crackle and you'll smell that toasted fragrance to let you know they are ready. Remove from the heat.

To assemble the salad, layer the roasted parsnips and pears on a large platter, followed by the macadamias, toasted coriander seeds, herbs, lentil sprouts and flowers, if you have them. Combine the dressing ingredients and drizzle over the salad. Season to taste and serve.

WEEKLY ROAST

Chapter Four

I'm not always organised enough to prepare meals ahead of time; I had to accept long ago that's it's just not how my life works week to week. But what I *can* manage to regularly incorporate into my cooking schedule is a weekly vegie roast. Every Sunday I simply put all the vegies we haven't eaten throughout the week in a roasting tin and bake them, providing the basis for all sorts of wonderful meals — soups, salads, risotto, pasta, pasties, curries and even breads — in the days that follow.

Having roasted vegies already waiting in the fridge is a great way to put yourself ahead of the 'what's for dinner?' curve, but also ensure nothing goes to waste — because you don't always need the prettiest vegetables to make the tastiest meals.

Roasted Vegetable Pasties

Makes 4 pasties

980 g (2 lb 3 oz) mixed
roasted vegetables,
at room temperature,
cut into 2 cm (¾ in)
cubes (for the photo I've
used fennel, potato and
brussels sprouts)

3 g (2 teaspoons)
chopped lemon thyme

3 g (2 teaspoons)
chopped fresh sage

almond or soy milk,
for brushing

tomato sauce, to serve

SPELT PASTRY

240 g (8½ oz) plain
(all-purpose) white
spelt flour, plus extra
for dusting

25 g (1 oz) extra virgin
coconut oil

5 g (1 teaspoon) salt

75–90 ml (2½–3 fl oz)
water, enough to pull
dough together

Without a doubt, homemade pasties are a brilliant thing to have on hand —
or even better, in hand. And if you do a weekly roast using lots of different
vegetables, then pasties become fast-food options — fast, just not junky. Fast
whole food can be a thing if it's broken down into sizeable chunks throughout
the week.

Make a weekly vegie roast a part of your meal prep, and all of a sudden
roast vegie pasties are making a regular appearance. You can use any roasted
vegies in these pasties. Potatoes, fennel, brussels sprouts, pumpkin (winter
squash), cauliflower and even beetroot work well — just don't go for anything
with too much liquid, like tomatoes.

The pastry is really quick to prepare, and versatile too. I use it for samosas,
pies, 'sausage' rolls — anything pastry wrapped.

Preheat your oven to 180°C (350°F).

Combine the roasted vegetables in a large bowl with the fresh herbs. Stir
together and season to taste with salt and black pepper.

To make the pastry, combine the flour, coconut oil and salt in a food processor
and blitz for 30 seconds. Slowly add a little water at a time until the dough
pulls together to form a ball.

Place the ball of pastry on a floured board and cut into four even pieces.
Have a small bowl of water ready to dip your fingers into.

Using a rolling pin, roll one pastry piece out into a circle about 20 cm (8 in)
in diameter. Place one-quarter of the filling mixture in a small mound along
the centre line, tapering off at each end. Use your fingers to wet the edges
of the pastry. Pull the two sides over the filling and press together using your
index finger and thumb, to concertina the join, working all the way around
to each end. Finally, fold the very last piece of dough at each end over itself,
to completely seal the pasty.

Repeat with the remaining dough and filling to make four pasties. Brush a little
milk across the top of the pasties.

Bake for 25–30 minutes, or until the pastry just starts to colour and is cooked
on the bottom. This is not the kind of pastry that puffs up, so don't wait for that
as a sign it's ready.

Remove from the oven and slide onto a wire rack, to ensure your pasties don't
end up with soggy bottoms. Nothing worse.

We always eat ours with Dad's homemade tomato sauce. Not sure they
can be called pasties without sauce!

Roasted Eggplant & Black Tahini Baba Ghanoush

Makes about 300 g (10½ oz)

GLUTEN FREE

750 g (1 lb 10 oz) whole eggplants (aubergines), roasted (see tip)

130 g (4½ oz) black tahini

45 ml (1½ fl oz) lemon juice

30 ml (1 fl oz) extra virgin olive oil

30 g (1 oz) flat-leaf parsley

3–4 garlic cloves, peeled

8 g (1½ teaspoons) salt

5 g (2 teaspoons) smoked paprika

TO SERVE

seeds from ½ pomegranate (optional)

20 ml (½ fl oz) extra virgin olive oil

My adoration for baba ghanoush sits in the same space many people assign to hummus. I absolutely love hummus too, but try as I might, I've never been able to grow enough chickpeas for even a teacup's worth of hummus — whereas eggplants seem to like our Mediterranean climate in the Barossa, turning into megaliths in our garden in a matter of days if we're not harvesting them regularly. In summer I always throw eggplants into the oven when I'm doing my weekly roast, because that really is the only thing you need to consider ahead of time if you want to have this moody-coloured, smoky-flavoured dip on hand throughout the week.

I initially made this with black tahini only because I'd run out of white tahini, but as soon as I saw it in the food processor, I decided it was a keeper for its dramatic colour alone. Fresh pomegranate seeds add delicious sweetness, but if you don't have any, please make the dip regardless. It's so good with chunks of fresh sourdough, or spread across a bagel as part of a burger ensemble. I know you'll come up with so many ways to eat this.

Cut the roasted eggplants in half. Scrape the flesh into a food processor, discarding the skins. Add the remaining ingredients and blitz until smooth, but not liquid; it's fine to have some texture from the parsley and eggplant.

To serve, spoon some of the baba ghanoush onto a plate. Scatter with the pomegranate seeds, if you have them, and drizzle with the olive oil.

Store any remaining baba ghanoush in an airtight container in the fridge and enjoy within 3–4 days.

tip ——— to roast whole eggplants

Leaving the skin on the eggplants, prick them with a fork three or four times across each side. Place on a baking tray and roast in a preheated 200°C (400°F) oven for 50–60 minutes, or until the eggplants have started to sink in on themselves and are soft all the way through.

Roasted Grapes with Almond Ricotta on Sourdough

*Serves 2 as part of
a light brunch*

GLUTEN FREE
(with gluten-free bread)

1 kg (2 lb 4 oz) table
grapes, any variety

40 ml (1¼ fl oz) extra
virgin olive oil

5 g (1 teaspoon) salt

15 g (½ oz) fresh
rosemary sprigs

2 slices Sourdough
Bread (page 58)

40 g (1½ oz) Almond
Ricotta (page 227)

Although I grew up among grapevines in the Barossa, with my parents both working in the wine industry, we never really ate a lot of local grapes, as they were almost exclusively grown for wine. When we bought our farmhouse, everyone asked if we were going to plant a vineyard, and while I can see the romance in that notion, I was only interested in planting vines so I could eat the grapes!

And that's exactly what we did, starting with sultana grapes and beautiful big red seedless grapes, as well as a few varietals that have seeds, because although it's annoying to have to eat around them, their flavour is worth it. What I didn't bank on was just how prolific the harvest would be from only a few grapevines — I guess vines really are in their happy place in the Barossa.

We eat as many grapes as we can straight from the bunch. I also juice some, and love having them in salads. In my quest to avoid wasting any of our bounty, I came across the idea of cooked grapes in dishes such as schiacciata, which I love making with a sourdough base. Grape pizza is not necessarily a fast thing, though, so when I added some less than perfect grapes into my weekly roast, this quick brunch idea came about.

You'll have plenty of leftover roasted grapes to add to other dishes such as salads, curries and Persian-style rice dishes. The leftovers will keep in an airtight container in the fridge for up to a week.

Preheat your oven to 200°C (400°F).

Spread the grapes on a baking tray in a single layer. Drizzle with the olive oil and sprinkle with the salt. Poke the rosemary sprigs in among the grapes.

Roast for 20 minutes, or until the grapes are nicely puckered and just starting to split. If you overcook them, they'll become jam. I always err on the side of undercooking — that way they keep their shape, too.

Toast your sourdough slices and spread with the almond ricotta. Top with the roasted grapes, drizzle with the olive oil and serve immediately, while your toast is still nice and crunchy.

Roasted Olives with Orange & Rosemary

Makes about 250 g (9 oz)

GLUTEN FREE

300 g (10½ oz) whole
brined olives, unpitted

60 g (2 oz) fresh
rosemary sprigs

5–7 garlic cloves
(20 g/¾ oz), unpeeled

30 ml (1 fl oz) extra
virgin olive oil

zest of 1 orange,
cut into 2–3 cm
(¾–1¼ in) strips

5–8 fresh thyme sprigs

5–8 fresh marjoram
sprigs

We've been brining our own olives ever since we moved back to the Barossa, with the first years' harvests entirely foraged from roadside trees. More recently, our own grove of olive trees has provided us with enough olives for the year, so we've had time to get to know the particular varieties we're growing, rather than the hard and fast approach needed when you forage from a dry-grown tree of unknown cultivar.

In those early days of hits and misses in our brining technique, the best kind of Plan B emerged in the form of roasted olives. Any time we had to pull out olives that weren't quite right — too soggy, too split, too salty — we simply put them in the oven to roast and they morphed into something I can't give up now. Regardless of whether we need to remedy any preserving mistakes or not, roasted olives are always on the menu.

This recipe is also a simple way to make store-bought olives 'bespoke', even if you don't have olive foraging and brining plans on your to-do list. You can use any type of olive, and also mix different types together. If you're buying them, I'd still recommend going for unpitted olives, because I feel there's a sense of ritual involved in rolling an olive seed around in your mouth; it's a flavour reward for effort. That, and they look more like you've just foraged them!

Preheat your oven to 200ºC (400ºF).

Spread the olives on a baking tray that has sides high enough to catch the juices and oil as they roast.

Add half the rosemary sprigs, keeping the rest for serving. Add the garlic cloves and drizzle with the olive oil.

Roast for 20–30 minutes, until the olive skins are just starting to pucker. Remove from the oven.

Remove the rosemary, replacing it with the reserved fresh sprigs. Pop the garlic cloves from their skins, leaving them whole. Stir them back through the olives, along with the orange zest strips, thyme and marjoram.

Serve immediately, with fresh sourdough bread to soak up the roasting juices and oil.

Spelt Samosas with Peas, Roasted Potato & Seasonal Masala

Makes 10 small samosas

40 g (1½ oz) Wholefood Vegie Stock Paste (page 232)

10 g (2 teaspoons) finely grated fresh ginger

30 g (1 oz) Spring Masala mix (page 241)

10 g (2 teaspoons) tamarind purée

25 g (1 oz) extra virgin coconut oil

100 g (3½ oz) red-stemmed silverbeet (ruby chard), leaves washed and cut into 2 cm (¾ in) strips

80 g (2¾ oz) shelled fresh peas (or frozen peas)

250–280 g (9–10 oz) roasted potatoes (see tip), cut into 1 cm (½ in) cubes

15 g (½ oz) coriander (cilantro) leaves

My brother has been responsible for some of my favourite food memories. He has an uncanny knack of leading me into unexpected situations that require another folder be added to the archive of all things delicious. Our sibling food moment that inspired this recipe was actually in a food court. My brother has taken me to some seriously dodgy places — yet regardless of how uninspiring the surrounds may be, he comes up with the flavour goods time and again.

The food court in question is smack-bang in the middle of Bangkok, nine floors up into the clouds of smog, atop a department store full of more stuff than any one person could possibly need in a lifetime.

The scene initially played out like so many others, with me whingeing about wanting to eat mango on the street under the tree near our restaurant. The whingeing continued on the train, through the rotating doors of the department store, through the perfume section and all the way up the escalators to the cashier. My brother disappeared into the abyss of shoppers all looking for their favourite thing for lunch. I sighed like a spoilt brat and started to bumble my way into the crowd.

And there they were, two super-smiley faces behind a wall of samosas and a cauldron of chai tea. Three minutes later, I walked back to my brother with a plate of fresh samosas, a huge pot of chai tea and a completely different attitude.

Samosas and chai — so good. A sip of tea and a nibble of spicy samosa, and so it went for the next few minutes. My brother didn't say a word as I talked about how the heat of the tea perfectly amplified the spice in the samosas, and how incredible the pastry was, and how I would never again eat samosas without drinking chai at the same time. Another favourite food memory to recreate as soon as I arrived home.

These samosas make the most of fresh spring peas and silverbeet from our garden, along with potatoes from our weekly roast. I've used a 'spring masala' inspired by Ayurvedic principles, but any of the masala mixes on page 241 would also work well.

There's no deep-frying with these... so while the samosas are baking, make a big pot of Stovetop Chai (page 50) to enjoy with them when they've just come out of the oven.

SPELT PASTRY

240 g (8½ oz) plain
(all-purpose) white
spelt flour

25 g (1 oz) extra virgin
coconut oil

5 g (1 teaspoon) salt

75–90 ml (2½–3 fl oz)
water, enough to pull
dough together

In a small bowl, mix the stock paste, ginger, spring masala mix and tamarind purée into a paste.

Add the coconut oil to a large frying pan over high heat. Immediately add the spice paste and stir to prevent sticking. Cook the paste for 30 seconds. Add the silverbeet and peas, continuing to stir for 2–3 minutes until the silverbeet wilts and the peas are cooked. Stir the roasted potato cubes through to coat with the paste and create an even mix of vegetables.

Remove from the heat, stir the coriander through and season with salt to taste. Allow to cool while you prepare the pastry.

Preheat your oven to 180°C (350°F). Line a baking tray with baking paper, or lightly dust with flour.

To make the pastry, combine the flour, coconut oil and salt in a food processor and blitz for 30 seconds. Slowly add a little water at a time until the dough pulls together to form a ball.

Divide the pastry into five equal balls. Working with one pastry ball at a time, roll them out to a thin disc about 20 cm (8 in) in diameter. Cut each disc in half to create 10 half-moons. Place a couple of heaped tablespoons of filling in the centre of each crescent, then pull the sides over the filling, sealing them at the base of the samosa. (No need to moisten the edges with water; you can just press the dough together with your fingers.)

Place the samosas on the baking tray. Bake for 15 minutes, then turn the samosas over and bake for a further 15 minutes to brown the other side.

Serve warm, with copious amounts of chai tea. Nibble and sip.

tip ——— to roast potatoes

Cut the potatoes into quarters and place on a baking tray. Drizzle with 50 ml (1¾ fl oz) extra virgin olive oil and season with salt and black pepper. Roast in a preheated 200°C (400°F) oven for 30–40 minutes, or until the potato is tender and starting to caramelise along the edges.

Hand-Rolled Cavatelli with Roasted Fennel, Pine Nuts & Lemon

Serves 4

20 g (¾ oz) pepitas (pumpkin seeds)

1 batch of Sourdough Pasta Dough (page 80), rested and at room temperature

60 ml (2 fl oz) extra virgin olive oil

40 g (1½ oz) Wholefood Vegie Stock Paste (page 232)

600 g (1 lb 5 oz) fennel, roasted (see tip)

100 g (3½ oz) pine nuts

3 g (1 teaspoon) lemon zest (preferably from a Meyer lemon)

30 ml (1 fl oz) lemon juice (preferably from a Meyer lemon)

3 g (2 teaspoons) marjoram leaves

5 g (4 teaspoons) fennel fronds (if available)

2 g (2 teaspoons) rocket (arugula) flowers (if available)

It's hard not to see food as therapy when the making of it requires enough of your attention that your thoughts can't run away with you, but also just the right amount of familiarity to give you the confidence to leave any clear space free for daydreaming. Cavatelli-making is therapy. And I know I'm not the only one to think so, after watching a workshop of pasta enthusiasts in our stable kitchen who, after very successfully making ravioli, went home and hand-rolled cavatelli with their leftover dough, just for the fun of it.

I really love making ravioli, but I would make cavatelli far more often, as the process is a little faster and less exact, and great as a mid-week option, whereas I really see ravioli as a weekend project.

The texture of these little guys is deliciously springy, so we often have them with a very simple Roasted Tomato Passata (page 134)... but if you've already made this dough and have it sitting in the fridge, along with vegies from your weekly roast, here's another wonderful combination that comes together in no time at all (pictured on page 121).

You might like to add a few dollops of Almond Ricotta (page 227) to this at the table, if you haven't already had it in every meal this week!

Toast the pepitas in a dry frying pan over high heat for a minute or two, until they start to pop. Remove from the heat and set aside to cool and crisp up.

Once your pasta dough is at room temperature, you can shape it into cavatelli. You'll need a wooden butter pat, gnocchi pasta board or something with a ridged surface. Also, it's a good idea to line a baking tray with baking paper, to hold all the cavatelli in a single layer without them sticking, and make it easier to slide all the cavatelli into boiling water when it comes time to cook the pasta.

Pull off pieces of dough the size of a blueberry and roughly roll into balls. Using your thumb, press and roll one ball of dough away from you across the pasta board so it is imprinted on the outside by the ridges of the pasta board, and curls in on itself just a little.

Once you have made all the cavatelli, bring a large pot of water to the boil. The cavatelli will only take about 5–7 minutes to cook; have everything else ready, so you can quickly cook the sauce while the pasta is boiling.

Add the cavatelli to the boiling water, stirring gently to stop the pasta sticking. Leave to simmer rapidly for 5–7 minutes, or until they float to the surface. Once cooked, simply drain the pasta and leave to sit for a moment in the colander while you finish pulling the sauce together.

While the pasta is boiling, add the olive oil and stock paste to a medium saucepan over high heat. Cook the stock paste for a minute, stirring often.

Add the roasted fennel, pine nuts and lemon zest. Cook for a further 2–3 minutes, until the fennel is heated through and the pine nuts are starting to colour. Stir the lemon juice through and remove from the heat.

Add the hot cooked cavatelli to the pan with the toasted pepitas and marjoram, gently stirring to combine. Season to taste with salt, add the fennel fronds and rocket flowers if you have them, and serve immediately.

tip ——— to roast fennel

To roast the fennel, cut the bulbs into quarters lengthways. Place on a baking tray and drizzle with 50 ml (1¾ fl oz) extra virgin olive oil. Season with salt and black pepper and roast in a preheated 200ºC (400ºF) oven for 30–40 minutes, or until tender and starting to caramelise along the edges.

Roasted Mushroom Pâté

*Makes 2 small cups
of pâté*

300 g (10½ oz) Swiss
brown mushrooms
(if unavailable, use field
mushrooms instead)

15 ml (3 teaspoons)
extra virgin olive oil

5 g (1 teaspoon) salt

30 g (1 oz) garlic cloves,
unpeeled

175 g (6 oz) black beans,
cooked or tinned

15 ml (3 teaspoons)
mirin

10 ml (2 teaspoons)
tamari

3 g (2 teaspoons) fresh
marjoram

2 g (2 teaspoons) fresh
thyme leaves

1 g (½ teaspoon) freshly
ground black pepper

30 g (1 oz) extra virgin
coconut oil, melted

2 fresh bay leaves

If ever there was an elusive foraging fixation, it's mushrooms. Every time there's rain, followed by a little sunshine, followed by more rain, I'm always wondering if mushrooms might be rearing their pretty heads somewhere in our paddock. We have a few mushroom rings (fairy rings!) that have repeated their offerings, but it's never something to rely on, and therein lies my obsession, I suppose.

I love mushrooms. Everything about them. Their tenacity in literally being able to push through the earth, their beautiful neutral colour palette, and their incomparable flavour. I could romance the idea of field-picked mushrooms forever, but their elusive nature means most of our mushrooms are bought from the farmers' market or greengrocer — and, if given the choice, Swiss browns are always my first.

Having said that, this mushroom pâté was originally made with field mushrooms and came about because I couldn't walk past them when I saw them in my horse's paddock. They were definitely a little battle-weary after being nibbled at by bugs, so they were destined for either soup or pâté. I had my weekly roast happening and added them to the mix, drizzling them with a little olive oil and sprinkling them with salt. Everything deepens when you roast mushrooms — their flavour, their colour and their magical smell.

Combined with black beans, they make quite a dramatically coloured pâté. I love serving it as a 'ploughman's lunch' with lots of sourdough, some olives, Almond Ricotta (page 227) and Pickled Fennel Flowers (page 170). Those lucky ploughmen.

Preheat your oven to 200°C (400°F).

Place the mushrooms caps down, stems up, in a baking dish big enough to hold them all in a single layer. Drizzle the olive oil over the mushrooms and sprinkle with the salt. Scatter the garlic cloves among the mushrooms.

Roast for 15 minutes, then remove from the oven.

When the garlic cloves are cool enough to handle, slip them from their skins, popping the roasted cloves into a food processor. Add the mushrooms, black beans, mirin, tamari, marjoram, thyme and pepper, as well as any roasting juices from the mushrooms. Blitz until smooth, but still a little textured.

Spoon the mixture into two serving cups, smoothing the tops. Pour a layer of melted coconut oil over each, then gently press a bay leaf on top of each cup.

Immediately place in the fridge to set the coconut oil and seal the pâté against oxidisation. The coconut oil mimics the more traditional layer of lard or duck fat used with meat-based pâtés.

If you'd rather eat the pâté immediately and skip the coconut oil, that's fine too. Sealed with coconut oil, the pâté will easily keep in the fridge for up to 1 week.

Roasted Brussels Sprout Salad with Snow Peas, Apple & Chervil

Serves 4

GLUTEN FREE

60–80 g (2–2¾ oz) rocket (arugula), with flowers if possible

400 g (14 oz) brussels sprouts, roasted (see tip)

150 g (5½ oz) snow peas (mange tout), with tendrils if possible, halved lengthways

1 apple (100 g/3½ oz), thinly sliced

50 g (1¾ oz) Baby Red Lentil Sprouts (page 242)

10 g (⅓ oz) chervil leaves

50 ml (1¾ fl oz) extra virgin olive oil

20 ml (½ fl oz) lime juice

10 g (2 teaspoons) Green Gomasio (page 234)

It's been so satisfying watching poor old brussels sprouts going from the least chosen thing on a menu to being a prime indicator of food cool. I'll be darned if we can grow them, though, here on our hill! Each year I come running in from the vegie garden or glasshouse to report the first signs of the little globes appearing, and every year they seem to press pause at that moment in time, leaving us with lots of very small, very loose little 'cabbages'. I still eat them... but then I go and get the 'real' ones from people at the farmers' market who seem to know the magic incantation needed for growing sprouts.

Snow peas, on the other hand, have found a great deal of happiness in our glasshouse over the years, evening out our brussels growing disappointment, and also giving me the chance to add their curly little tendrils to our plates.

On a large platter, layer the rocket leaves and roasted brussels sprouts, followed by the snow peas and apple slices. Scatter the lentil sprouts and chervil across the salad.

Drizzle the olive oil and lime juice over. Sprinkle with the gomasio and season with salt to taste.

tip —— to roast brussels sprouts

Cut the brussels sprouts in half lengthways. Place on a baking tray, drizzle with 50 ml (1¾ fl oz) extra virgin olive oil and season with salt and black pepper. Roast in a preheated 200°C (400°F) oven for 30–40 minutes, or until tender and starting to caramelise along the edges.

Risotto of Roasted Beetroot, Balsamic & Toasted Cumin Seeds

Serves 4

GLUTEN FREE

8 g (4 teaspoons) cumin seeds

1.5 litres (52 fl oz) water

50 ml (1¾ fl oz) extra virgin olive oil

400 g (14 oz) arborio rice

45 g (1½ oz) Wholefood Vegie Stock Paste (page 232)

450 g (1 lb) beetroot, roasted (see tip), then cut into 2–3 cm (¾–1¼ in) pieces

20–30 ml (½–1 fl oz) balsamic vinegar

25 g (1 oz) Turmeric Butter (page 230)

50 g (1¾ oz) Almond Ricotta (page 227)

Risotto is another reason to love the idea of a weekly roast. There's something far fancier about risotto made with caramelised, deeply flavoured and richly coloured roasted vegies. Years ago I made a beetroot risotto for a Christmas menu at Eat Me. The first attempt with grated raw beetroot gave the celebratory colour I was hoping for, but completely lacked flavour. Then we tried roasting the beetroot first, and adding it to the risotto as it was cooking — so much better, with exactly the sweet, earthy flavour you'd expect from beetroot. No amount of stock or salt can stand in for that beautiful concentration of roasted flavour, so I almost always roast vegies before making any risotto now.

Make sure your favourite music is playing, so you can enjoy the time spent stirring for the next 20–25 minutes. Toast the cumin seeds in a dry frying pan over high for a minute or two, until they start to pop. Remove from the heat and either leave whole, or roughly grind into a textured powder using a mortar and pestle. Set aside.

In a saucepan, bring the water to the boil, then keep it at a constant simmer.

In a separate large saucepan, stir the olive oil, rice and stock paste continuously over high heat for 1–2 minutes. Add the roasted beetroot pieces and stir for another minute, before adding the first ladleful of boiling water. (Remember, you don't need to use liquid stock here, because you already have the concentrated fresh stock paste in the pan, so the water will turn it into liquid stock as you cook — another reason I love this stock paste so much.)

Add the boiling water a ladleful at a time, stirring constantly until each ladle of liquid is absorbed. Don't rush this process. It's the slow absorption of liquid that gives risotto that classic creamy texture. Stay with the risotto, stirring constantly, until all the liquid has been absorbed and the rice is cooked, but still 'al dente'.

Cover the pan and let the risotto sit for a few minutes to become extra creamy Remove the lid. Stir the balsamic vinegar through to taste, then the butter, to give a final gloss to the dish. Serve immediately, topped with dollops of almond ricotta and sprinkled with the toasted cumin seeds.

tip —— to roast beetroot

Cut the beetroot (peeled or not — I never do) into quarters lengthways and place on a baking tray. Drizzle with 50 ml (1¾ fl oz) extra virgin olive oil and season with salt and black pepper. Roast in a preheated 200°C (400°F) oven for 30–40 minutes, or until tender and starting to caramelise along the edges.

Cauliflower Soup with Macadamia Parmesan

Serves 6–8

GLUTEN FREE

8 g (2½ teaspoons) yellow mustard seeds

25 g (1 oz) Turmeric Butter (page 230)

45 g (1½ oz) Wholefood Vegie Stock Paste (page 232)

800–900 g (1 lb 12 oz– 2 lb) cauliflower, roasted (see tip)

700 g (1 lb 9 oz) potatoes, roasted (see tip)

2.5 litres (87 fl oz) water

30 g (1 oz) Macadamia Parmesan (page 231)

extra virgin olive oil, for drizzling

rocket (arugula) flowers, if available

I will never forget our first home-grown, hand-picked cauliflower. It barely resembled the giant, super-white specimens on offer in a shop, but it was held aloft in triumph, regardless. It was a little on the small side, and bound to continue shrinking even more if left to the fat green grub that was sharing it with us, leaving a trail of chewed destruction in his wake — and making that cauliflower an obvious choice for the soup pot. Our brassica gardening efforts have evolved enormously over the years (thank you, grub-eating runner ducks), but I haven't changed this soup recipe since I first made it.

Roasting vegies — especially cauliflower — before they go into a soup makes every difference to the depth of flavour. And when you start doing your weekly vegie roast-up, you're bound to come up with lots of new soup ideas — they pretty much make themselves when you have different roasted vegies already waiting in the fridge.

Soup season is a great time to start making the fresh Wholefood Vegie Stock Paste on page 232, if you haven't already. I know you'll use it for so many dishes besides soups; it's the quiet achiever of recipes in this book.

Toast the mustard seeds in a dry frying pan over high for a minute or two, until they start to pop. Remove from the heat and grind into a powder using a mortar and pestle.

Melt the butter in a large soup pot. Pan-fry the stock paste and roasted cauliflower and potatoes over high heat for 2 minutes to cook the stock paste. Stir the freshly ground mustard seeds through. Pour in the water to cover, bring to the boil, then leave to simmer for 5 minutes, or until all the ingredients are piping hot.

Remove from the heat, then purée the soup with a hand-held blender until smooth and creamy. Check the seasoning and add salt to taste.

Serve the hot soup, sprinkled with the macadamia parmesan, drizzled with olive oil, and garnished with rocket flowers if you have them.

tip —— to roast cauliflower & potatoes

Cut the cauliflower into 3–4 cm (1¼–1½ in) pieces and place on a baking tray. Cut the potatoes into quarters and place on a separate baking tray. Drizzle each tray of vegies with 50 ml (1¾ fl oz) extra virgin olive oil, then season with salt and black pepper. Place the trays in a preheated 200°C (400°F) oven. Roast until tender and starting to caramelise along the edges — the cauliflower will take 20–30 minutes, and the potatoes 30–40 minutes.

Roasted Pumpkin Rotolo
with Crispy Sage

Serves 4–6

200 g (7 oz) Almond Ricotta (page 227)

700 g (1 lb 9 oz) pumpkin (winter squash), roasted (see tip)

FRESH PASTA DOUGH

340 g (11¾ oz) plain (all-purpose) white spelt flour

3 g (½ teaspoon) salt

pinch of ground turmeric, for colour (optional)

15 ml (½ fl oz) extra virgin olive oil

165–175 ml (5¼–5½ fl oz) water

Admittedly, rotolo is not a quick dish. The satisfaction of making something delicious for those you love is time well spent — so I would like to fly the flag for slowing things down a bit, just every now and again, to really immerse ourselves in flavour and aroma and the craft of creating something that nourishes all of our senses.

Spend the morning making rotolo and then, when you bring it to the table for Sunday lunch, let time slow down again, so you can make the most of the crowd going wild! It's quite the dramatic reveal when you pull the wrapped rotolo from its bath, cut the string trussing it, and then finally peel the cloth away from the cooked pasta. All that steam is like a smoke machine on a stage before the performance begins. Don't serve this while you're hidden in the kitchen is what I'm trying to say: this is a dish to share, from start to finish.

I've included a fresh pasta dough recipe here, in case sourdough pasta (page 80) isn't your thing, so feel free to use it as your regular fresh pasta mix if that works better for you.

To make the pasta dough, place the flour, salt and turmeric (if using) in a food processor. Add the olive oil and water in a steady stream while the processor is running. Mix until the dough begins to form a ball. If the dough seems too dry, add a few drops of water at a time. If the dough is too wet, add a pinch of flour at a time until it becomes more workable.

Once the dough comes together, remove from the processor bowl and form into a ball. Wrap the dough in plastic wrap and leave to rest in the fridge for 20–30 minutes. (You will have left-over dough to keep in the fridge for fettuccine or spaghetti later in the week, as you'll likely use one-third of this pasta for the rotolo.)

Using a pasta machine, roll out three pieces of the rested dough into three rectangles measuring about 35 cm x 15 cm (14 in x 6 in), and no more than 5 mm (¼ in) thick.

Spread a clean tea towel on the bench and place each sheet of pasta on it, overlapping the pieces by about 1.5 cm (⅝ in). Seal the pieces across the two joining seams by pressing the pasta together with your fingers. Cut the short edges to even up the joined sheet of pasta.

Starting at the long side closest to you, spread the almond ricotta evenly across two-thirds of the joined pasta sheet. Arrange the pumpkin pieces on top of the ricotta. Season with salt and black pepper.

CRISPY SAGE

60 g (2 oz) Turmeric
Butter (page 230)

10–12 sage leaves

OPTIONAL GARDEN EXTRAS

rocket (arugula) flowers

dill sprigs

marjoram leaves

Using the tea towel to help you, roll the rotolo away from you. The filling will push over into the final third of the rotolo as you continue to roll; don't worry, you'll have plenty of pasta to make the final join. When you get to the end of the roll, wet the long edge with a little water and seal the rotolo. Seal each of the short ends in the same way. Firmly wrap the rotolo in the tea towel and use string to secure it from end to end, like a big sausage (see photos on page 132).

Fill a fish poacher, or the biggest pot you have, with water, and bring to the boil. Lower the wrapped rotolo into the boiling water and cook at a rapid simmer for 30–35 minutes.

Remove from the pot and allow to cool a little before snipping the string and gently unwrapping the rotolo. The rotolo can be sliced into about 5 cm (2 in) portions and placed on a warm platter while you add the finishing touches.

To make the crispy sage in browned butter, add the butter to a small saucepan over high heat, then drop the sage leaves in — they'll sizzle a little. Stir them around for 30 seconds and then spoon the hot, browned butter and sage leaves over cut portions of the rotolo.

Top with extra herbs, salt and black pepper to serve.

tip ——— to roast pumpkin

Peel the pumpkin and cut into 2–3 cm (¾–1¼ in) chunks. Place on a baking tray and drizzle with 50 ml (1¾ fl oz) extra virgin olive oil. Season with salt and black pepper. Roast in a preheated 200°C (400°F) oven for 30–40 minutes, or until tender and starting to caramelise along the edges.

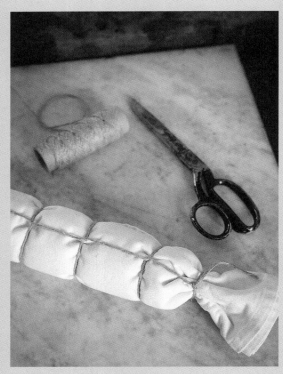

Roasted Tomato Passata

Makes about 3 kg
(6 lb 12 oz)

GLUTEN FREE

3 kg (6 lb 12 oz)
tomatoes, washed
and left whole

40 ml (1¼ fl oz) extra
virgin olive oil

1 whole garlic bulb
(60 g/2 oz), skin on,
separated into cloves

30 g (1 oz) fresh
rosemary sprigs, leaves
stripped off the stems

5 g (1 teaspoon) salt

I made the mistake of making this passata for an Italian friend who was staying with us and he nearly had kittens. So, a warning to traditionalists: I've cooked the tomatoes in this passata. Please don't hate me!

My second mistake was saying that I actually had no idea it was such a big deal. Then I told him I just went with a technique that was most convenient for me, one I could fit into a busy working week. Yep, I just kept digging that hole. Although a traditional passata is based on raw tomatoes being plunged into boiling water and then being skinned, sieved and bottled, my method means I actually make passata regularly throughout our tomato season — far better than being deprived of homemade pasta sauce altogether.

My friend actually loved the pasta we made with the sauce, but we agreed I wouldn't call it passata anymore. Weeks later, we laughed at our whole conversation and the serious business of tomato sauce. Sometimes I'll be chatting to his wife on the phone and he'll sing out in the background that I better not be cooking my tomato sauce again. He has the best sense of humour — extra dry. He'll wonder why there's a page missing when I send him a copy of this book.

This sauce will keep in the fridge for several weeks in an airtight jar... or you can do what my mum does and freeze it. We'd best not mention that to my friend either.

Preheat your oven to 200°C (400°F).

Spread the tomatoes across a baking tray in a single layer and drizzle with the olive oil. Scatter the garlic cloves among the tomatoes, poke the rosemary sprigs in between, then sprinkle the salt across everything.

Roast for 30 minutes, or until the skins of the tomatoes are starting to blister. Remove from the oven and cool slightly.

When the garlic cloves are cool enough to handle, slip them from their skins, popping the roasted cloves into a food processor. Add the roasted tomatoes, rosemary leaves, and any roasting juices from the tomatoes. Blitz until smooth, but not completely without texture; you want sauce, not soup.

Enjoy with pasta dishes such as Sourdough Pasta (page 80) and Baked Pasta Shells Stuffed with Almond Ricotta (page 227), or as a sauce for a pizza base.

SHARED TABLE

Chapter Five

There are so many food stories set on the stage of a shared table. To me, it's the reason for all the growing, harvesting, preserving, cooking and foraging — the chance to share it. There's every opportunity to gather together for good food: birthdays, long weekends, the change of season, the mere fact it's Sunday, or a particularly generous bounty of homegrown tomatoes needing to be picked — it all ends up with a long table of enthusiasm for the simple act of eating together.

These are the recipes I rely on to not only feed a decent gathering of family and friends, but to do so in a way that either allows most of the prep to be carried out ahead of time, or calls on crowd participation, which sets such a lovely mood of pooled efforts to be celebrated once everyone sits down to eat.

Lettuce & Tarragon Soup

Serves 4–6

300–500 g (10½ oz–
1 lb 2 oz) lettuce, such
as cos or iceberg (any
variety that doesn't
have a bitter edge)

20 g (¾ oz) French
tarragon leaves, plus
extra to garnish

20 g (¾ oz)
chervil sprigs

50 ml (1¾ fl oz) extra
virgin olive oil

40 g (1½ oz) Wholefood
Vegie Stock Paste
(page 232)

25 g (1 oz) plain
(all-purpose) flour

1 litre (35 fl oz) water

For me, the time of year when summer is holding hands with autumn is so, so lovely. The sun becomes golden rather than blazing, and every night is a good night for sleeping. I especially look forward to that first drenching rain of the season, bringing with it a green peach fuzz that covers the hills where the harshness of late summer stood only days before. It's amazing how reassuring that first tinge of green can be, because in the midst of summer's searing heat there are times I can't imagine anything growing, ever again, in the endless red dirt. But along comes autumn... and then *shazam!* Green.

I've been making this soup for what seems like forever. I love the way it mimics the weather, but in a bowl — that 'neither hot enough for cold soup, nor cold enough for hot soup' kind of thing. Because the ingredients are so simple, you want the best version of them, so please do wait for the most beautifully fresh tarragon — really and truly French tarragon — to appear. I'm not going to harp on about growing your own herbs again, but I might just mention how easily French tarragon can be grown in a pot on a windowsill or city apartment balcony. I'd maybe go so far as to say, grow tarragon just so you can make this soup!

I make best use of the last of our cos lettuce each season, but this is just as delicious with iceberg or even a mix of lettuce leaves.

Roughly chop the lettuce and herbs. Set aside.

Heat a large saucepan. Add the olive oil and fry the stock paste over medium heat for 1 minute, stirring constantly, before adding the flour. Continue to stir, then gradually add the water, keeping the mixture as smooth as you can.

Bring to the boil and add the lettuce and herbs. Simmer for about 15 minutes, or until the lettuce is almost translucent.

Using a hand-held blender, process until smooth.

Season to taste with salt and black pepper. Serve topped with extra tarragon, and perhaps an extra drizzle of olive oil.

Cacao Mole with Borlotti Beans

Serves 4–6

GLUTEN FREE

375 g (13 oz) dried
borlotti beans

40 g (1½ oz) raw
almonds

3 black peppercorns

3 cloves

1 star anise

40 g (1½ oz) sesame
seeds

3 long red dried chillies
(10 g/⅓ oz)

3 g (1 teaspoon) smoked
paprika

3 g (1 teaspoon) sweet
paprika

3 g (1 teaspoon) ground
cinnamon

10 g (3 teaspoons)
raw unsweetened
cacao powder (or
Dutch-processed cocoa
powder if you prefer)

15 g (½ oz) rapadura
sugar

40 ml (1¼ fl oz) extra
virgin olive oil

40 g (1½ oz) Wholefood
Vegie Stock Paste
(page 232)

I had a thought about jet lag when we arrived home from Mexico after our first trip to the Yucatan Peninsula: perhaps the icky feeling is because your heart isn't quite ready to let go of the experiences you've had on your adventure away, rather than sitting in a plane for nearly 30 hours. This is clearly not a logical explanation, but it resulted in me bringing as much of the Yucatan home to our farm in the Barossa as possible. Surprisingly, it isn't that hard to blend those two worlds. Both are grounded in crossover produce like tomatoes, capsicums (peppers), almonds and beans — exactly the ingredients for the famous cacao mole we saw on menus everywhere, which I translated into a plant-based version using some of our homegrown vegies and chillies, and using the highly nutritious form of raw cacao powder we ate in Mexico, rather than the Dutch-processed cocoa I only knew from adding to cakes.

If you've never tried mole before, I understand the hesitancy. The idea of using chocolate in savoury dishes never really appealed to me before we visited Mexico — and that's after seeing one of my all-time favourite films, *Like Water For Chocolate*. I'm happy to admit I had it wrong. Cacao gives this dish its earthy, rich undertone and really lets the deeper flavour come through, rather than imparting the sweetness we typically associate with chocolate.

This isn't a fast recipe, but one to enjoy setting an afternoon aside for. The individual steps are like the scenes in a film — all smoky and slow-cooked and heady with spice. I first made this for a New Year's Eve dinner and it brings back the best memories... both of Mexico, and of a summer's night under the stars with friends out here on our hill. Food is magical like that.

You can easily make a double batch, keeping the capsicum quantity the same, freezing half for later, then adding more freshly charred capsicum when you're ready to serve.

Soak the borlotti beans overnight in plenty of cold water. Next day, drain the beans, add them to a saucepan and cover with plenty of fresh water. Bring to the boil, reduce the heat and cook at a rapid simmer for about 30 minutes, until only just tender. Drain and set aside.

Toast the almonds, peppercorns, cloves and star anise in a dry frying pan over high heat for 3–5 minutes, until the almonds are nicely toasted, stirring frequently so they don't burn. Add the sesame seeds and chillies and dry-roast, stirring, for a further 2 minutes, until the sesame seeds start to crackle. Remove from the heat and tip into a mortar or a food processor. Add the smoked and sweet paprika, cinnamon, cacao powder and sugar and grind or blitz to a fine powder.

Add the olive oil to a large saucepan and fry the stock paste for 1–2 minutes, until fragrant. Add the spice mixture and stir to distribute evenly.

300–400 ml
(10½–14 fl oz) water

350 g (12 oz) tomatoes,
chopped

280 g (10 oz) whole
yellow or red capsicums
(peppers)

lime wedges, to serve

Immediately add the water, tomatoes and drained borlotti beans, stirring until well combined. Simmer over low heat for 30–45 minutes, to allow the flavours to really meld together. Check the seasoning and add salt to taste, if needed.

While the mole is simmering, char the capsicums. Leaving them whole, place them over a direct flame and roast for 10–15 minutes, rotating often, until all sides are evenly charred and the capsicums are cooked through. Don't worry about how blackened they'll get — this develops the flavour in the flesh and you'll be peeling off the charred skin. (If you don't have a gas cooktop, you can always use your oven grill/broiler to char the capsicums. Just keep an eye on them, and constantly rotate them so they cook evenly.)

Place the charred capsicums in a paper bag and seal. Let them sweat for 10–12 minutes; you'll then find it very easy to slip off the blistered skins. Rinse off any remaining burnt bits. Cut the stems off and slice the flesh into 2 cm (¾ in) wide strips, discarding the seeds.

Serve the mole topped with the capsicum strips, with lime wedges on the side. I love serving it with polenta, homemade tortillas and grilled corn on the cob.

Sourdough Calzone with Kale, Olives & Potato

*Makes two 25 cm (10 in)
calzones; serves 4–6*

400 g (14 oz) potatoes,
washed

300 g (10½ oz) kale

60 g (2 oz) olives

20 g (¾ oz) mixed
fresh herbs, such as
marjoram, rosemary,
basil, thyme

15 ml (½ fl oz) extra
virgin olive oil

30 g (1 oz) Wholefood
Vegie Stock Paste
(page 232)

CALZONE
SOURDOUGH

80 g (2¾ oz) sourdough
starter, fed the night
before with 100 g
(3½ oz) each flour
and water
(see Language of
Sourdough, page 54)

250 ml (9 fl oz) water

8 g (1½ teaspoons) salt

330 g (11½ oz) plain
(all-purpose) white
spelt flour, plus extra
for rolling

Do you ever make dinner based on using lots of what you have on hand, regardless of whether the ingredients seem like they'll taste good together? I do. Winter is the time when we have kale going wild in the garden and jars of recently harvested olives, so all it took for this recipe to come together one freezing-cold afternoon was a little digging for potatoes.

'Pioneer cooking', I call it, because I often imagine those who have lived before us in our 175-year-old farmhouse at times scratching together a dinner plan that didn't involve a quick trip to the supermarket. Admittedly, they probably didn't have kale or olives either, but this serendipitous combination of a few simple ingredients makes for a delicious survival plan.

Kids love getting involved with the dough-rolling and potato treasure hunt, too, so I've made this many times when friends have come for a lazy weekend meal and no one is in any hurry to leave.

You will need to start this recipe the day before, in order to feed your sourdough starter with 100 g (3½ oz) water and 100 g (3½ oz) flour, so it's ready to use the following morning. This times nicely with having calzone for dinner or a late lunch.

If you have some Roasted Tomato Passata (page 134), definitely use that in lieu of making the fresh tomato sauce below. You can also use the sourdough as a pizza base; it should yield three 20 cm (8 in) round pizzas.

I never peel potatoes — even when making mashed potato — because I love adding the extra fibre and nutrients in their skins to my cooking, but by all means peel the potatoes if you'd prefer.

Make sure your sourdough starter has been fed the night before with 100 g (3½ oz) each flour and water, so it's ready to go for your calzone dough.

To make the dough, mix together the sourdough starter, water and salt in a large bowl. Add the flour and continue to stir, to ensure there are no pockets of dry flour in the mix. Cover and leave at room temperature, turning it over every 30 minutes, for the next 1½ hours, as per the instructions for making bread (page 58). Leave to prove until the dough has increased in volume by at least one-third. This usually takes 4–5 hours, depending on the ambient room temperature.

While the dough is proving, prepare the filling. Boil the potatoes until tender, then drain and leave to cool before cutting into 1.5 cm (⅝ in) cubes. Strip the stems from the kale and discard; cut the leaves into 2 cm (¾ in) strips. Pit the olives, then cut in half. Roughly chop the herbs.

QUICK TOMATO SAUCE

10 ml (2 teaspoons) extra virgin olive oil

500 g (1 lb 2 oz) tomatoes, roughly chopped

20 g (¾ oz) Wholefood Vegie Stock Paste (page 232)

Place a large saucepan over high heat and add the olive oil and stock paste. Stir for a minute or two, then add the kale and olives. Cook, stirring, until the kale has wilted, but still retains some texture; it will cook further in the oven. (You may need to wilt the kale in batches, depending on the size of your saucepan.) Mix the potato chunks through, then set aside to cool.

When the dough is ready, preheat your oven to 200°C (400°F). Flour a baking tray large enough to hold two 25 cm (10 in) calzones. Imagine a 25 cm (10 in) diameter pizza folded in half, into a half-moon — you'll have two of these.

Flour a board and cut the dough into two equal portions. Roll one half out with a rolling pin, into a round about 25 cm (10 in) in diameter and 5–8 mm (¼–⅜ in) thick. Place on the baking tray and spoon half the filling onto one side of the round, leaving a 2 cm (¾ in) border free of filling. Flip the other side of the dough over the filling and press the edges together, crimping them to ensure the calzone is completely sealed. Repeat with the remaining dough and filling to make the second calzone.

Bake for 30–35 minutes, until the dough is cooked through and nicely browned on top. Remove from the oven and leave to sit while you prepare the tomato sauce.

Simply combine all the tomato sauce ingredients in a saucepan and cook, stirring often, for 5–8 minutes, until the tomatoes have broken down and the sauce is hot.

Place the calzones on a serving plate and ladle an equal amount of tomato sauce over each. Season with salt and freshly ground black pepper and serve immediately.

I like to take the whole calzones to the table and cut into them there, releasing all their steamy goodness and allowing everyone to express their preference for more or less crust.

Smoked Almond Ricotta Gnocchi with Garden Herb Salsa Verde

Serves 2–4

30 g (1 oz) Turmeric Butter (page 230)

40 ml (1¼ fl oz) extra virgin olive oil, or to taste

fresh fennel pollen and fronds, to garnish (optional)

GNOCCHI

200 g (7 oz) Almond Ricotta (page 227)

10 ml (2 teaspoons) liquid smoke

110 ml (3¾ fl oz) water

5 g (1 teaspoon) salt

125 g (4½ oz) unbleached plain (all-purpose) white spelt flour, plus extra for dusting

SALSA VERDE

30 g (1 oz) fresh herbs, such as thyme, rosemary, oregano, mint

10 g (2 teaspoons) capers

If you've never made gnocchi before, start here. Possibly my favourite thing about this gnocchi is how foolproof it is. I know that term gets bandied around a lot, but I'm not kidding when I say this recipe has been made under serious duress with very little concern for any precision of method, and always turns out delicious. I've made it in swelteringly hot marquees during cooking demonstrations, I've made it on live TV when I realised I didn't have batteries in my scales until it was too late, and I've made it with kids of all ages who were doing everything to avoid following any kind of directions. It can also be made gluten free, using the Gluten-Free Flour Blend on page 245.

This is a gnocchi that requires no dexterity of any kind, if you'd like to start with very simple hand-cut portions, rather than rolling them over a pasta board in a more traditional manner. They'll even bob to the top of the cooking water to tell you when they're ready to scoop out!

The Smoked Almond Ricotta is also delicious in sandwiches and salads, on bagels, and stirred through pasta with garlic, chilli and extra virgin olive oil, but for this recipe you could just as easily use the classic Almond Ricotta on page 227 and omit the liquid smoke.

To make the gnocchi, put the almond ricotta in a bowl and, using a fork, mix the liquid smoke through until evenly dispersed. Add the water and salt and stir again, making sure there are no obvious lumps. Once smooth, add the flour and mix thoroughly.

Turn the dough out onto a well-floured surface and form into a rough log. Cut the log into four equal pieces. Roll each piece into a long sausage about 1.5 cm (⅝ in) thick. Cut into 2 cm (¾ in) pieces and lightly roll in flour. (If you have a wooden pasta board, you can gently roll the individual pieces along it, to score the traditional indented lines on the outside of the gnocchi.)

Bring a large pot of water to the boil over high heat to cook the gnocchi.

While you're waiting for the water to boil, make the salsa verde by finely chopping the herbs and capers together. This shouldn't be done too far ahead of serving, to avoid oxidisation of the herbs. (If you do need to make the salsa ahead of time, be sure to cover it with plenty of olive oil to stop the air discolouring the herbs; you want them to be vibrantly green.)

When your pot of water has come to the boil, add the gnocchi and cook for 3–5 minutes, or until all the gnocchi have risen to the surface.

Drain the gnocchi and return to the pan. Stir the butter and salsa verde through, along with olive oil to suit your taste.

Serve dusted with fresh fennel pollen and garnished with fronds, if available.

Spelt Dumplings with Nettle & Green Miso Broth

Makes 12–16 dumplings; serves 4

cabbage leaves, to line a bamboo steamer (optional)

extra virgin olive oil, for greasing

pea flowers and tendrils, to garnish (optional)

SPELT DUMPLING DOUGH

340 g (11¾ oz) plain (all-purpose) white spelt flour

165–175 ml (5¼–5½ fl oz) water

15 ml (½ fl oz) extra virgin olive oil

3 g (½ teaspoon) salt

NETTLE FILLING

150 g (5½ oz) freshly picked unsprayed nettles (or baby spinach, if unavailable)

30 g (1 oz) Wholefood Vegie Stock Paste (page 232)

I'd hate for you to miss out on these dumplings due to very good weeding techniques at your house... so if you don't have nettles growing wild, you can easily substitute baby spinach. Nettles are a weed, but one I'm happy to see pop up around our sheds and in the vegie garden when spring arrives each year. Nettles provide a decent dose of vitamins A, K and D, as well as iron and calcium, among other nutrients. Pretty amazing little 'weed', really.

Rest assured that the cooking process will break down the fine hairs on the leaves, and I promise you won't have any stinging as you swallow! You'll absolutely need to be sure the nettles haven't been sprayed, so that will likely rule out any roadside foraging, but almost anyone who has a healthy garden will be only too happy to share their nettles. I usually pick nettles with gloves to avoid the stings — or you can go in with intent, if you have the skill to 'grasp the nettle'. That's a life lesson in itself.

If you're wondering what nettles taste like, I can only get close to describing their unique flavour as 'verdantly green'. They taste of spring to me: full to the brim of life force. I make nettle powder each year by dehydrating the leaves, then blitzing them in my food processor, so I can add the powder to smoothies all year round, but they are all the better when they're freshly picked.

These dumplings are one of my favourite — and quite literal — versions of paddock-to-plate fare. This dish comes together quite quickly, particularly if you have already discovered the Staple Provisions chapter and have Wholefood Vegie Stock Paste and Green Miso Paste on hand.

Place the dough ingredients in a food processor and mix until the dough comes together. Set aside to rest while you prepare the filling.

Bring a large pot of water to a boil and blanch the nettles on their stems for 1 minute. Drain them in a colander and leave to cool while you roll out your dumpling wrappers.

The easiest way to roll the dough is to use a pasta machine, working the dough to setting 5, or as thick as you would for fresh ravioli — about 3 mm (⅛ in) thick. If you don't have a pasta machine, you can absolutely roll the dough out by hand; it will just take a bit longer. Only use flour to help with rolling the dough if it's absolutely necessary. You don't want to dry the dough out before it goes into the steamer.

Once you've rolled the dough out, use a 6–8 cm (2½–3¼ in) cookie cutter, or drinking glass, to cut out 12–16 uniform circles, placing them on a sheet of baking paper.

GREEN MISO BROTH

4 tablespoons
(75 g/2½ oz) Green Miso
Paste (page 233)

750 ml (26 fl oz) boiling
water, approximately

Once the nettles have cooled, finish preparing the filling. Roughly chop the nettles and place in a bowl, then mix the stock paste through.

Place a heaped teaspoon of the filling in the centre of each round of dough and pull up the sides of each wrapper to seal the dumplings. Really press the dough together with your fingers, using a folding method on one side of each dumpling to 'pleat' the dough and create the classic half-moon dumpling shape.

Bring a pot of water to the boil. Line a bamboo steamer with baking paper, or cabbage leaves, if you have them, poking a few air holes in the leaves or paper with a chopstick. Rub a little olive oil on the bottom of each dumpling before placing them in the steamer, to help stop them sticking as they cook, and making sure they don't touch each other — again to prevent sticking. Depending on the size of your steamer, you may need to cook the dumplings in two batches.

Cover the steamer and set the basket over the pan of boiling water. Steam the dumplings at a rapid simmer for 12 minutes, or until the dough becomes shiny and is cooked through.

Meanwhile, bring a kettle to the boil. Prepare the miso broth by placing 1 tablespoon of green miso paste in four serving bowls and mixing 185 ml (¾ cup) boiling water into each bowl.

Place three or four steamed dumplings in each bowl of hot broth. Top with pea flowers and tendrils, if you have them, and serve immediately. You could always garnish with fresh coriander (cilantro) leaves or even snow pea (mange tout) sprouts instead.

Baked Pasta Shells Stuffed with Almond Ricotta & Roasted Tomatoes

Serves 4–6

GLUTEN FREE

700 g (1 lb 9 oz) Roasted Tomato Passata (page 134)

300 ml (10½ fl oz) water

200 g (7 oz) conchiglioni pasta shells (about 24 shells)

250 g (9 oz) Almond Ricotta (page 227)

2 g (1 teaspoon) pink peppercorns

3 g (¾ teaspoon) salt, to taste

20 ml (½ fl oz) extra virgin olive oil

Comfort food usually means something baked, and often something creamy; this pasta recipe gets big ticks in both those boxes. Really, though, I consider all food a comfort. I love eating food, growing food and harvesting it. Bringing it inside and preparing it with other ingredients — all while smelling the fragrance of fresh vegies and herbs, knowing how much I'm going to love the moment I bring the fork to my mouth as the final punctuation in this incredible alchemical process we call 'eating'. Maybe that's a bit deep, but let's blame gardening and the connection it gives us to our food. That level of gratitude makes for the best kind of eating, don't you think?

If you haven't made the Almond Ricotta yet, this recipe might be the deciding factor to go ahead and soak some almonds. You'll use the ricotta in so many recipes, but it's especially delicious in this dish. Comforting, some might say...

Preheat your oven to 200°C (400°F). Have a large baking dish at the ready — ideally one measuring about 30 cm x 24 cm (12 in x 9½ in), and about 8 cm (3¼ in) deep.

Mix the tomato passata and water together in a bowl, then pour half the liquid into the baking dish.

Using a teaspoon, fill the uncooked pasta shells with the almond ricotta. Arrange the filled shells in the baking dish, facing upwards, to keep the ricotta in place, and making sure the pasta shells fit snugly.

Gently pour the remaining tomato passata mixture in and around the pasta shells. Do this as slowly as you can, to avoid disrupting the ricotta too much. The liquid should just cover the tops of the filled shells. Sprinkle the pink peppercorns and salt over the top and cover the baking dish with foil.

Turn the oven down to 190°C (375°F) and bake the shells for 1 hour. Carefully remove the foil and bake for a further 10–15 minutes, or until the shells are starting to colour along their edges.

Remove from the oven and allow to sit for 10 minutes before serving, giving time for the pasta to absorb any residual liquid. The tomato sauce should be lovely and thick around the cooked shells.

Drizzle the olive oil over the cooked shells and serve. I love having a big salad of fresh rocket (arugula) leaves on the side.

Yellow Tomato & Eggplant Curry

10 g (3 teaspoons) coriander seeds

6 g (3 teaspoons) cumin seeds

6 black peppercorns, whole

4 cloves

3 g (1 teaspoon) sweet paprika

3 g (1 teaspoon) ground turmeric

25 g (1 oz) Turmeric Butter (page 230)

45 g (1½ oz) Wholefood Vegie Stock Paste (page 232)

500 g (1 lb 2 oz) eggplants (aubergines), cut into 2 cm (¾ in) pieces

500 g (1 lb 2 oz) yellow tomatoes, roughly chopped

30 g (1 oz) fresh ginger, peeled and grated

80–125 ml (2½–4 fl oz) water

30 ml (1 fl oz) lemon juice

30 g (1 oz) basil leaves (preferably purple basil, if available)

5 g (1 teaspoon) salt, or to taste

One of the best aspects of having a vegie garden is that whatever might be going gangbusters in your garden is likely to be different from the produce thriving in a friend's garden, so you can fill in the gaps for each other. I remember saying that I couldn't wait to move to the country so I could be that person who puts apricots or lemons in a bag for visitors as they're leaving, insisting they take some zucchini, too, because we can't possibly eat them all. It's such an incredibly precious thing to me. If you gave me your new puppy that you just picked up, it would be on a par with how I feel about being gifted brown paper bags full of hand-nurtured cucumbers and tomatoes from friends' gardens. We're talking serious appreciation.

One Saturday morning, homegrown eggplants arrived across our trestle at the farmers' market –and I couldn't have been more grateful. These eggplants were the lovely long type, perfect to cut through into chunks and still melt down beautifully when cooked. At the time we had yellow tomatoes growing like weeds in our garden and this curry basically made itself. This is such a simple recipe, but it really packs a flavour punch — as long as the produce is great to begin with. Broken-record clichés of recipe writing, I know, but it makes every difference.

Toast the coriander seeds, cumin seeds, peppercorns and cloves in a dry frying pan for a minute or two, over medium heat, until they start popping and smell incredible. Remove from the heat, add the paprika and ground turmeric and grind to a powder using a mortar and pestle or spice grinder.

Heat the butter in a saucepan and add the stock paste. Fry for 1 minute over medium heat, stirring often, before adding the eggplant, tomatoes, ginger and your freshly ground spice mix. Stir well for 3–5 minutes, until the juices start coming out of the tomatoes and the eggplant is just starting to soften around the edges. Depending on how juicy the vegetables are, you may need to add some or all of the water to stop the curry sticking.

Bring to the boil, then reduce the heat to medium–low. Cover and simmer for about 15 minutes, until the eggplant is tender.

Remove from the heat, then stir in the lemon juice, basil and salt. I love serving this curry with brown basmati rice, homemade naan bread and coconut raita.

Brown Rice Kitchari with Seasonal Masala

Serves 4

GLUTEN FREE

500 g (1 lb 2 oz) seasonal mixed vegetables, such as potatoes, cauliflower, spinach, green beans, tomatoes, peas, eggplant (aubergine)

25 g (1 oz) Turmeric Butter (page 230)

45 g (1½ oz) Wholefood Vegie Stock Paste (page 232)

25 g (1 oz) Winter Masala mix (page 241)

30 g (1 oz) fresh ginger, peeled and grated

20 g (¾ oz) fresh turmeric root, peeled and grated

200 g (7 oz) medium-grain brown rice

100 g (3½ oz) dried black lentils

400 g (14 oz) tinned tomatoes

750 ml (26 fl oz) water

5 g (1 teaspoon) salt, or to taste

TO SERVE

30 g (1 oz) coriander (cilantro) leaves

coconut yoghurt (optional)

hemp seeds (optional)

Here's a crowd-pleaser for you. One that can work to use whatever vegies you love, and leave out those you're not so fond of. That might translate into making best use of a bumper crop of spinach, beans and potatoes when eggplant (aubergine), tomatoes and peas aren't in season. This is another dish that offers an element of crowd participation, if that's an option, but then mostly cooks itself while you chat with friends. It's an all-in-one kind of dish, too, so you can bring it to the table and everyone can help themselves, adding coconut yoghurt if they choose, or upping the chilli to taste.

Kitchari sits in the same place as stew for me, so it immediately heads to the top of my comfort food list, and is a delicious option for a winter get-together. I've used a winter masala spice mix here, but you can also use any of the masala spice blends on page 241, depending on the season. Any leftovers are just as good reheated the next day.

Prepare your chosen vegetables, cutting the larger ones into 2–3 cm (¾–1¼ in) chunks. Set aside.

Melt the butter in a saucepan over high heat. Fry the stock paste, masala mix, ginger and turmeric for 1–2 minutes, stirring continuously.

Add the rice and lentils, and any potato chunks, if using. Stir to coat in the paste, then pour in the tomatoes and water. Bring to the boil, reduce the heat to medium and put the lid on. Simmer for 25–30 minutes.

Add the chopped vegetables, put the lid back on and cook for a further 10 minutes, to allow the vegetables to steam through with the rice. Check the rice and lentils are cooked, and add extra water if further cooking time is required.

Season to taste with the salt. Serve topped with coriander, and coconut yoghurt and hemp seeds if desired.

Spanakopita of Garden Greens

Serves 4–6

120 g (4 oz) frozen filo pastry (about 8 sheets)

1 kg (2 lb 4 oz) mixed greens, such as cavolo nero, silverbeet (Swiss chard), spinach, curly kale

40 g (1½ oz) fresh herbs, such as marjoram, rosemary, thyme, parsley

100 g (3½ oz) kale tips, if available

45 g (1½ oz) Wholefood Vegie Stock Paste (page 232)

30 ml (1 fl oz) extra virgin olive oil

200 g (7 oz) Almond Ricotta (page 227)

5 g (2½ teaspoons) smoked paprika

80 g (2¾ oz) Turmeric Butter (page 230)

Anything baked in pastry will always get my attention, especially in winter when our vegie garden is groaning with greens — spinach, cavolo nero, silverbeet (Swiss chard) and curly kale are punctuated by bunches of parsley, marjoram, thyme and rosemary, and they all go into this spanakopita in varying ratios.

A more recent discovery has been kale tips — the little green buds that form as kale cycles through its growing stages. If you catch them before they bloom into little yellow flowers, they are so good in any recipe that calls for greens. For a few years now, I've purposely been allowing some kale plants to go 'to seed' just so I can get my hands on these little tippy bits to use in pasta dishes, soups, salads and even on top of pizza. Don't worry, this recipe will certainly still meet your daily chlorophyll requirements without them, but if you are growing kale in your garden, it's a chance to enjoy these little flower buds, rather than see their emergence as a sign the plant has reached the end of its life cycle. They're another gift from the garden that can't be found in stores, making them all the more precious — another reason to grow a little patch of homegrown greens.

Thaw the pastry on the bench, under a damp tea towel so it doesn't dry out.

Preheat your oven to 200°C (400°F). Dig out a pie dish or enamel pan, ideally measuring about 32 cm x 20 cm (13 in x 8 in), and about 6 cm (2½ in) deep.

Remove the larger, tougher stems from the greens. Roughly chop the leaves into strips about 2 cm (¾ in) wide. Finely chop the herbs and mix together with the chopped greens and kale tips (if using).

Heat a large saucepan and fry the stock paste in the olive oil for 1–2 minutes, stirring often. Add the chopped greens and herbs; you may need to do this in batches, to fit all the greens in your pan. Continue cooking to wilt the greens down, stirring to make sure they don't stick to the bottom of the pan. As soon as the greens have softened, but before the mixture is mushy, remove from the heat and stir the almond ricotta and paprika through. Set aside to cool.

Melt the butter in a small pan over high heat. Brush your pie dish with the melted butter. Lay two filo sheets across the base and up the sides. Brush those pastry sheets with melted butter. Lay another two sheets on top, at a right angle. Brush those with butter and place another two sheets on top, again at a right angle.

Fill the pastry with the cooled greens and ricotta mixture. Sprinkle with salt and black pepper. Wrap the pastry over the mixture, like an envelope, sealing with a little more melted butter; if you like, you can scrunch up the last two sheets of filo, to make the top of the pie a little fancier. Brush the top of the pastry with more melted butter. Add a final sprinkle of salt and pepper.

Turn the oven down to 180°C (350°F). Bake the spanakopita for 20–25 minutes, until nicely browned. Serve hot, while the pastry is still lovely and crisp. It's wonderful with the Purple Carrot, Fig & Pearl Barley Salad on page 98.

Whole Miso-Roasted Cauliflower

Serves 6-8

GLUTEN FREE

1 whole cauliflower, about 550–600 g (1 lb 4 oz–1 lb 5 oz)

150–200 g (5½–7 oz) Green Miso Paste (page 233)

20 ml (½ fl oz) extra virgin olive oil

OPTIONAL EXTRAS

fresh herbs

lemon wedges

toasted seeds

coconut yoghurt

roasted chickpeas

This may not be the first time you've come across the idea of whole roasted cauliflower, but I am sharing this recipe because it takes delicious advantage of having Green Miso Paste (page 233) on hand. The only real preparation, once the miso paste has been made, is to massage it all over the cauliflower before roasting it. This whole roasted cauliflower is quite the centrepiece when it arrives on the table, no matter what occasion you have gathered for, and the age of your guests has no bearing on how many eager volunteers will help work the gooey miso paste into the cauli; it's irresistible crowd participation!

If you would like to add further layers, you could top the roasted cauliflower with coconut yoghurt, toasted seeds, roasted chickpeas and fresh herbs. And the giant pearl couscous known as moghrabieh makes an excellent side dish, if you can find it. You can't really go wrong — another reason to have this roasting away in the oven while you enjoy chatting to everyone before sitting down to eat.

Be sure to set your oven racks to allow plenty of space for the cauliflower in the roasting pan *before* you preheat your oven, otherwise you'll be juggling hot metal before you even starting cooking — not something you want to do in front of guests, speaking from experience.

Preheat your oven to 200°C (400°F). Line a roasting pan with baking paper.

Remove any green leaves from the cauliflower, but leave the base intact.

With clean hands, rub the green miso paste all over the cauliflower. Be generous with the amount of paste, and really spend some time massaging it into all the bumps and crevices.

Place the whole cauliflower in the roasting pan. Drizzle with the olive oil and roast for 40–50 minutes, or until a fork can easily pierce the middle of the cauliflower. (If your cauliflower is browning too quickly and it's still a way off being cooked, cover it with foil, then remove the foil for the final 10 minutes of roasting time.)

Remove from the oven, dress with your choice of optional extras and bring to the table to carve and serve immediately.

Tofu Noodle Soup

Serves 6–8

500 g (1 lb 2 oz)
Sourdough Pasta Dough
(page 80), rested and at
room temperature

50 g (1¾ oz) Wholefood
Vegie Stock Paste
(page 232)

50 ml (1¾ fl oz) extra
virgin olive oil

400 g (14 oz) carrots,
grated

400 g (14 oz) celery, with
leaves, chopped

2 litres (70 fl oz) water

200 g (7 oz) Homemade
Tofu (page 236), cubed

30 g (1 oz) flat-leaf
parsley, chopped

5 g (1 teaspoon) salt,
or to taste

This is the chicken noodle soup of my childhood, without the chicken. It still has everything you want in a soup, though, and has been a regular winter standby, especially as it's also the perfect way to use our less-than-gorgeous-looking carrots and celery that are nevertheless full of homegrown flavour, having battled the conditions here. I find it amazing how the more plants need to rally themselves against the elements, the stronger their flavour. There's something in that...

This soup comes together quickly, especially if using store-bought tofu and udon or soba noodles. When we have friends or family coming for a meal, I love making the noodles, because it's another chance for everyone to get involved if they want to. The scene usually ends up with me and a bunch of kids on the noodle-making team, while everyone else wanders around the garden picking parsley. This recipe is really just a basic guide for you to add whatever herbs or vegies take your fancy.

To me, when this soup pulls together homemade Wholefood Vegie Stock Paste (page 232), Homemade Tofu (page 236) and the homemade sourdough noodles in this recipe, it's still very much a special occasion meal, purely based on the time invested in the preparation. Your future self will thank you every time you reach for any of the Staple Provisions made in advance, making something as simple as this soup feel so much greater than the sum of its parts — my favourite kind of cooking.

I highly recommend serving this with a loaf of sourdough (page 58) and Turmeric Butter (page 230) — because soup is only a meal when there's bread and butter, don't you think?

Once your pasta dough is at room temperature, you can make the noodles with a pasta machine, or by rolling the dough out by hand using a rolling pin. I use the fettuccine attachment on my pasta machine, because I prefer the noodles a little bit thicker and flat, rather than thin and round like spaghetti. (Either will taste delicious, though! This is just a personal preference, based on childhood memories of the flat egg noodles my mum would use.) Set the noodles aside, loosely covered with a clean tea towel.

Heat a heavy-based saucepan over medium heat and fry the stock in the olive oil for 1–2 minutes, stirring often. Stir the carrot and celery through and cook for 2–3 minutes, before pouring in the water.

Once the soup has come to the boil, gently drop the noodles in and cook for 10–15 minutes, until the noodles are al dente.

Turn off the heat and add the tofu and parsley. Season with salt and black pepper to taste. Leave to sit for about 5 minutes before serving, as this soup really keeps its heat and I don't want anyone jumping in with all the excitement of a big appetite and burning their tongue! Serve with fresh bread and butter.

Garden Smorgastarta with Dill Cucumber & Pear

Serves 6–8

800 g (1 lb 12 oz)
Sourdough Bread
(page 58)

400 g (14 oz) pears

200 g (7 oz) Dill
Cucumbers with Green
Tea & Vine Leaves
(page 182)

350 g (12 oz) cucumbers

fresh herbs such as
dill, chervil and
marjoram (and pea
tendrils, if available)

400 g (14 oz) Almond
Ricotta (page 227)

OPTIONAL EXTRAS

capers

edible flowers

If ever there was a reason to have an afternoon tea, it's smorgastarta — the prettiest version of a cheese sandwich you'll likely come across. Smorgastarta takes the notion of cucumber sandwiches to a whole new realm; with pea tendrils trailing and edible flowers dotted across the top, it feels like something Alice would have eaten in Wonderland. Once you have made the Almond Ricotta (page 227) and you're looking for a new way to enjoy your freshly baked sourdough, put a guest list together and invite your friends over for tea. I promise everyone will be inspired to make their own version of this traditional Swedish sandwich cake.

You can layer your smorgastarta with all and any of your favourite sandwich ingredients. I find cucumber and pear a wonderful pairing — afternoon-tea-worthy of Jane Eyre herself.

Slice the crusts off the bread and reserve for another purpose. Cut the bread into eight slices of even thickness, about 10 cm (4 in) square.

Have all your sandwich ingredients ready before you start assembling. Thinly slice the pears, and cut the dill cucumbers into thin rounds. Using a mandoline, cut the fresh cucumbers lengthways into very thin slices, to wrap around the outside of the smorgastarta.

Lay your fresh herbs out on a plate, along with any other extras you've chosen to use as decoration on top.

To assemble the smorgastarta, place two slices of bread next to each other on the plate you would like to serve the sandwich cake on. These will be your rectangular base layer. Use a palette knife or flat, non-serrated butter knife to spread a layer of almond ricotta over the bread slices.

Add a layer of sliced pears on top of the first layer of bread. Lay another two slices of bread across the top, then spread with more almond ricotta.

Add a layer of dill cucumbers, followed by two more slices of bread. Spread more almond ricotta over the bread slices. Add another layer of pears, then finish with the final two slices of bread that will form the top of the sandwich cake.

Using flat hands, gently compress the sandwich cake from above to make sure all the ingredients have settled into their ricotta layers. Once you are happy that the sandwich cake is nicely squared up, with all the bread slices exactly on top of one another, and no filling spilling out the sides, you can start to 'ice' the sandwich cake with the remaining ricotta. Save the top until the final step, so you can hold the sandwich in place with your fingers on the top two slices of bread while you spread the ricotta around each of the four sides. Finally, ice the top of the cake with ricotta, to cover the entire sandwich cake.

Now you can decorate! This part of the process is completely bespoke, so let your imagination lead the way. I like to wrap the fresh cucumber slices around the outside of the sandwich cake, then add some herbs, flowers and pea tendrils for decorating the top of the finished smorgastarta.

The smorgastarta can be held in the fridge for up to 2 hours, but it's best not to leave it too much longer than that, or your beautiful artwork will start to wilt. I usually serve it immediately, cutting it at the table using a sharp serrated knife, and using a cake spade to serve it onto plates — just like a cake.

Pea & Tofu Curry

Serves 2–4

GLUTEN FREE

250 g (9 oz) Homemade
Tofu (page 236),
cut into 1.5 cm
(⅝ in) cubes

1 brown onion
(70 g/2½ oz)

25 g (1 oz) fresh ginger,
peeled

25 g (1 oz) coriander
(cilantro) sprigs

35 g (1¼ oz) Wholefood
Vegie Stock Paste
(page 232)

45 ml (1½ fl oz) extra
virgin olive oil

25 g (1 oz) Turmeric
Butter (page 230)

400 g (14 oz) tinned
tomatoes

200 ml (7 fl oz) water

400 g (14 oz) peas, fresh
or frozen

I've stolen this recipe from my husband. Without question, he's the 'Matar Paneer' guy in our house — and he was also that guy at our restaurant in Bangkok, where for years his matar paneer recipe featured on the menu. Back then it was more traditional, using cow's milk to make the paneer cheese, but after making our own tofu, we noted how similar the process is to making paneer — so it was an easy jump to 'matar tofu' from there.

I absolutely love this dish. It has so many great memories associated with it, throughout the recipe's evolution and our own. It will always remind me of our early days living in Melbourne, picking our own tomatoes on the rooftop of our rented terrace house to make the sauce for this curry (by all means use tinned tomatoes, though — it will be just as delicious and far easier). Then there were all the years I would walk into the Bangkok restaurant kitchen and smell it cooking and know exactly what I was having for dinner that night. And the first time we went to India, I loved watching it being served in so many different ways, all of them authentic, and all bearing little local tweaks. But in particular, I will never forget the one and only time the stars aligned for us to use our own homegrown tomatoes, homegrown peas (not a lot, but just enough) and homemade tofu, with fresh coriander (cilantro) from a friend's garden (ours had already bolted). It was quite amazing to find it had a flavour all of its own. Farmhouse flavour.

I've served this dish to so many people of very different tastes and ages, and have yet to see anyone deny the offer of a second helping — including my dad, who I firmly place in the fussy eater category. It's another crowd-pleaser, is what I'm trying to say.

If you'd like a firmer fried tofu in your curry, place the tofu cubes in a hot sandwich press for 2–3 minutes, then set it aside to stir through the curry just before serving. The tofu is equally delicious without this step, retaining its soft texture in the curry. I like it either way.

To make the masala, toast all the seeds and peppercorns in a dry frying pan over high heat for a minute or two, until the seeds start to pop and crackle in the pan. Remove from the heat, add the turmeric and paprika and grind to a powder using a mortar and pestle or a spice grinder. Set aside.

Combine the onion, ginger, coriander, stock paste and olive oil in a food processor and blitz until smooth.

In a large saucepan, melt the butter over high heat. Immediately add the onion paste and masala spice mix and fry for 1–2 minutes. Stir in the tomatoes and water. Bring to the boil and add the peas, then reduce the heat and simmer for 15 minutes, to thicken the sauce and cook the peas.

Remove from the heat. Stir the tofu and fresh tomatoes through and garnish with coriander. We always serve this curry with brown basmati rice. And I always overeat this curry. Every time. Just a warning.

MATAR MASALA

3 g (1 teaspoon) fennel
seeds

3 g (1 teaspoon) brown
mustard seeds

3 g (1 teaspoon) yellow
mustard seeds

8 g (4 teaspoons) cumin
seeds

10 g (3 teaspoons)
coriander seeds

1 g (½ teaspoon) black
peppercorns

3 g (1 teaspoon) ground
turmeric

1 g (½ teaspoon) hot
paprika

TO SERVE

2 fresh tomatoes
(150 g/5½ oz), chopped

coriander (cilantro)
leaves

FORAGED FOOD

Chapter Six

I purposely drive along a rotating collection of back roads according to the season, just to check on secret pockets of wild food as they briefly pop up, ripe for the picking. Abandoned orchards against ramshackle farmhouses, now populated by sheep; a small forest of pine trees in a creek bed; a smattering of truly dry-grown roadside olive trees; or grape vines too old for anyone to bother picking any longer — all offering the most intense flavour from their hard-won existence. I love the thrill of finding a tree before the birds do, especially in such hidden and beautiful locations, just as much as I love the chance to turn otherwise forgotten produce into food. There's something all the more precious about foraged food, perhaps because of the unlikely odds of finding it in the first place.

Wild Olives in Brine

For each 5 kg (11 lb) batch of fresh olives, you'll need a clean 10 litre (340 fl oz) food-grade bucket with a lid

GLUTEN FREE

fresh olives

water

rock salt

Apple Cider Vinegar (page 178)

extra virgin olive oil

There's a certain wild olive tree that grows near our farmhouse — not near enough that we can see it without taking a drive, but not too far that we can't check it weekly, and then daily, as olive-picking season approaches. I can't tell you where this tree is, because these kinds of secrets are fiercely guarded around here. I do know we're not the only ones privy to its location, because each year we vow to be the first to pick it, and each year we're pipped at the post and only manage to get the second helpings. Foragers can't always be choosers, so we're happy to walk away with any of this gnarly old tree's kalamata bounty — and with plenty of other wild olive trees along the same track, we always bring home several buckets of mixed olives to brine.

If you'd like to brine your own olives without access to wild or homegrown specimens, boxes of fresh olives can often be found at farmers' markets when the season rolls around, any time from late autumn through to early winter. The recipe below is based on ratios, so that you can adjust it according to the amount of olives you have on hand. I would suggest 5 kg (11 lb) is a minimum for the effort required, but any amount will feel worth it when you unseal that first jar of your own home-cured olives.

Pick over the olives to pull out any leaves that may have made it into the mix. We then use a sharp knife to cut a small slit in each olive to speed up the curing process.

Put the olives in your 10 litre (340 fl oz) bucket and fill it with fresh water. Leave the olives to soak for 3 days, then drain, refilling the bucket with fresh water and repeating the soaking/draining process for a total of three rounds. Make sure the olives are completely submerged in the water at all times; we place an upside-down plate on top of the olives in the bucket, then place the bucket lid loosely on top, to keep any bugs out but still allow the olives to breathe.

Once you have completed the fresh water soaking cycles, you can start the brining process. Mix up a salty brine solution in a ratio of 1:10 rock salt to water — for instance, 100 g (3½ oz) salt in 1000 g (1 litre/35 fl oz) water. Again, make sure the olives are completely covered with the brine solution at all times by weighing them down with a plate in the bucket.

Leave the olives in the brine for 1 week, then drain and repeat with a fresh batch of salt brine solution.

Repeat this process weekly with the salt brine for about 1 month, or until the olives have lost their bitterness. If you have cut little slits in your olives, they will likely be ready to put into jars after 4–6 weeks in the brine. If you haven't cut the olives beforehand, they can take a couple of months to lose their bitterness.

Once the olives have cured to your taste, drain and pack into sterilised jars. (I run all my jars through the dishwasher on its hottest cycle just before putting the olives in them.)

Once you have packed the olives into each jar, cover with a vinegar brine, made by adding 1 part apple cider vinegar to 3 parts salt brine — for instance, 250 ml (9 fl oz) vinegar and 750 ml (26 fl oz) salt brine.

Top each jar with a layer of olive oil before sealing.

Stored in a cool, dark place, the sealed olives will keep for at least 6 months, and will be ready to eat about 4 weeks after jarring.

tip ——— hold the 'extras'...

You can add orange or lemon zest, and/or fresh thyme or rosemary, or perhaps some roasted garlic with the vinegar brine, but in our experience it's always better to add any extras to your serving bowl of olives rather than during the jarring process. This helps enormously with avoiding the ultimate disappointment of proudly opening a jar of olives — only to find mould has paid an unwelcome visit.

Pickled Fennel Flowers

40–80 g (1½–2¾ oz) fresh fennel flowers or green seed heads

200 ml (7 fl oz) Apple Cider Vinegar (page 178)

80 g (2¾ oz) rapadura sugar (or raw sugar, if you prefer a paler pickling liquid)

Isn't it funny how things can come full circle? Years ago, the team from *Australian Country Style* magazine came to photograph our farmhouse and Lee Blaylock was the stylist in the team. It was the first time we'd met, and while we chatted and drank tea and worked through the list of shots needed for the article, Lee discovered my obsession with fennel and told me about the idea of pickled fennel flowers. At this stage I'd pickled everything else I could wildcraft — including baby pine cones, which Lee noticed on my pantry shelf, and which instigated our pickling conversation — so why not fennel flowers?

I really want you to be able to have these little flavour bombs in your life, so here is the basic pickling juice, and then I'll leave it to you and your garden to decide between pickling the fennel flowers or going for the green seed heads — both are delicious. You will likely have seen wild fennel on the roadside and wondered what could be done with those beautiful flower heads. Well, once you've checked to make sure they haven't been sprayed, you can simply pickle them and add them to salads and pizzas, or to serve as part of a cheese board, or let them go diving in a champagne flute of kombucha like I do.

Forgive me setting you on a pickling frenzy once these make their mark in your recipe repertoire. Actually, we can blame Lee for that! And at the same time, thank her for casually mentioning all those years ago that she would be the stylist on my cookbook if I ever had the chance to write one — and now she is. Full circles.

Place the fennel flowers or seed heads in a heatproof bowl.

Heat the vinegar and sugar in a saucepan and bring to the boil until the sugar has dissolved. Pour over the fennel.

Store in a sterilised jar. The pickles will keep for an age in a cool cupboard out of direct sunlight. They will be ready to eat after 3–4 weeks.

tip ——— *sterilising jars*

When pickling or making jams and the like, I simply run all my jars through the dishwasher on its hottest cycle just before filling them.

Preserved Lemons

*Makes 2 × 500 g
(1 lb 2 oz) jars*

GLUTEN FREE

250 g (9 oz) salt (I use
Celtic sea salt)

1–1.2 kg (2 lb 4 oz–2 lb
11 oz) lemons, unwaxed
and unsprayed

2 g (1 teaspoon) black
peppercorns

2–4 fresh or dried bay
leaves

50 ml (1¾ fl oz) extra
virgin olive oil

There are so many ways to prepare preserved lemons, and here is one of the easiest. The lemons used for preserving definitely don't need to be the prettiest, but avoid any that are soft or bruised. You want a lovely thick skin, full of essential oils — one of the reasons, I think, homegrown or foraged lemons are so well suited to preserving, because often they're all rind and not much flesh.

Our lemon trees now supply us with a regular haul of fruit, enough to allow for some to be preserved, but for years I relied on a friend's tree that magically grew with very little water or attention on the edge of their vineyard and would groan with fruit, offering plenty to jar up for the season. When citrus trees are happy, they let you know! So if you happen to be driving past a particularly laden tree on a country road, keep an eye out for an honesty box nearby and get ready to swoop.

After sterilising your jars (see tip, opposite page), pour a layer of salt into each, to cover the base.

Cut each lemon into quarters, leaving the skin on and not worrying too much about removing seeds. Add three or four lemon quarters to each jar, pushing them down with the end of a wooden spoon as you go, to release the lemon juice. Add another layer of salt for every three or four lemon quarters, packing the salt around them and continually pushing them down with the wooden spoon so that the salt and lemon juice covers the fruit.

To every layer of lemons, add a few black peppercorns and a bay leaf as you add the salt.

Pack as many lemon quarters into the jars as possible, so you end up with a snug fit to help keep the fruit submerged under the top layer of salt and juice. Finish with a layer of salt. Finally, pour the olive oil on the very top before sealing each jar with a lid.

Place the packed jars in a cool, dark spot in your pantry and leave to sit undisturbed for 10–12 weeks before eating. Once you have opened the lemons, it is best to store them in the fridge, adding more olive oil to the top of the jar each time you remove some lemon. This will help keep mould at bay, and stop the lemons oxidising.

To eat the preserved lemons, scrape the flesh away from the rind and discard. Cut the rind into small strips to use in risottos, dips, salads, pesto and the Preserved Lemon Hummus on page 32. You can use preserved lemon anywhere you would use olives.

Clockwise from top left: Wild Olives in Brine (page 168),
Preserved Lemons (page 171), Pickled Fennel Flowers (page 170),
Dill Cucumbers with Green Tea & Vine Leaves (page 182).

Wild Almond Butter

Makes about 3 cups of almond butter, equivalent to 3 × 250 ml (9 fl oz) jars

GLUTEN FREE

400 g (14 oz) raw almonds, with skin on

5 g (1 teaspoon) salt

10 ml (2 teaspoons) sweet almond oil (optional)

There's a gorgeous spot not far from our farmhouse that I aim to visit at least twice a year. It's a dirt road lined with wild almond trees, overlooking an old church, among vineyards and wheat paddocks. I love it. My first visit of the year is at the beginning of spring, to see blossom cotton-tailing across each almond tree. I always have a pair of secateurs in the car so I can jump out and gather a huge armful of blossoms to take home and put in vases. The blossoms drop all over the place, driving my husband crazy, but I can't resist how beautifully it marks the change of season.

My second visit is at the end of summer, as the last of the season's warmth passes the baton to cooler autumn days. I'm always so happy to pull up to these wizened old trees laden with nuts. I'm not the only one to wildcraft along this road, but when the season is in a giving mood, there are always plenty of almonds to go around. So when the going is good, I pick as many wild almonds as I can, then come home to start the process of shelling and roasting them to make this incredibly precious almond butter.

Preheat your oven to 170°C (325°F).

Place the almonds on a baking tray and roast for 8–10 minutes, or until toasty brown and smelling amazing.

Remove from the oven and allow to cool for 5 minutes. You just want them cool enough to handle; having them still warm will help the almonds release their oils when blending.

Add the warm almonds and salt to a food processor and blitz for 10 minutes. You might need to scrape the almond meal from the sides, but this is all you need to worry about with any kind of nut butter. Your food processor might get a little weary if it's as overused as mine, so rest it every 3 minutes or so, to avoid burning out the motor.

Once the almond meal has started to come together in a paste, you can add a little drizzle of almond oil if you'd like it to be a bit runnier. You can flavour nut butters with whatever takes your fancy at this final stage of blending; I've added lavender flowers and mandarin peel, or cinnamon and cacao — or just leave as is for a pure nutty taste. Either way, super good for you.

Pour the finished almond butter into jars and seal with a lid. It will keep unopened in the cupboard for up to 3 months. Once opened, refrigerate and use within 1 month.

Instant Verjuice

GLUTEN FREE

unripe green grapes

Some of you will know I worked with Barossa food legend Maggie Beer for a very long time... and in my mind, I can't mention verjuice without mentioning her. The first person to really shine a light on verjuice commercially in Australia, Maggie introduced so many people to this traditional grape product. I fell in love with it when I started working with her because it's such a great addition to cooking, giving a vibrancy to food in a similar way to lemon juice.

I certainly won't claim that my cheat's method below will result in the same verjuice Maggie makes, but it's a super-simple way to have that bright flavour addition on hand. All you need are unripe green grapes, a juicer and some ice cube trays — and then, when the mood for risotto, pasta, quinoa, soup, a salad dressing or fancy roasted vegies strikes, just pop in a couple of ice cubes from the freezer and you'll be singing the praises of verjuice! It's really good stuff.

Simply run the grapes through a juicer, pour the juice into ice cube trays and stash in the freezer. The freezing process stops the grape juice fermenting, keeping that wonderful bite. Use the verjuice wherever you'd use lemon juice or white wine in a recipe. I love drinking it with sparkling mineral water, too.

Rosehip Shrub

GLUTEN FREE

500 ml (17 fl oz) Apple Cider Vinegar (page 178)

450 g (1 lb) raw sugar

300 g (10½ oz) rosehips, stripped clean of leaves and stems

There is so much to be said for gathering roadside produce you might otherwise whiz past. Olives polka-dotting trees, golden quinces hanging like lanterns... and rosehips that announce their distinctive sweet–sour fragrance well before you spot their muted red tones. Shrubs of the non-bushy kind are a perfectly old-fashioned way to draw out and preserve the flavour of rosehips — as well as other fruits — in a vinegar-based syrup. Then all that stands between you and your inner mixologist is a bottle of bubbly water and a particularly pretty glass.

Bring the vinegar to the boil in a saucepan. Add the sugar and continue to boil until the sugar has dissolved. Remove from the heat and add the rosehips.

Pour into a large sterilised jar (see page 170) and cover with muslin (cheesecloth) or a clean tea towel. Leave to steep in a cool, dark place for 2–3 weeks.

Taste the syrup. If the rosehip flavour has steeped out enough for your liking, strain them out, pour the syrup into a large sterilised bottle and store in the fridge, where it will keep for more than 6 months. Add the shrub to soda water, kombucha or other drinks, in the same way you would a cordial.

Apple Cider Vinegar

GLUTEN FREE

apples, unwaxed and unsprayed

champagne yeast

vinegar 'mother' culture

I try not to have too many plans for Sundays beyond tea drinking and riding horses. And then, somehow or other, a farm project pops up, usually based on something that has to be done in our garden — or being handed produce from someone else's garden. That's how we ended up making apple cider vinegar for the first time, after being given a box of beautiful organic apples from a friend's orchard. We whip through apple cider vinegar like no tomorrow, so it gave us the perfect chance to put our finally renovated cellar to good use — which in itself was many Sundays' worth of previous farm projects.

Considering how long vinegar lasts, and how utterly satisfying it is using it in a salad dressing, you'll end up looking out for windfall apples sooner rather than later. If you are already into apple cider vinegar, you'll no doubt be familiar with the kind that has a vinegar 'mother' in the bottle. You can grow this, just like you'd grow a kombucha scoby. That will take a while — or you can find a friend who makes vinegar and barter with them for a mature mother, as we did.

The amount of yeast required will depend on the amount of juice you have. We made about 2 litres (70 fl oz) of juice from 5 kg (11 lb) of apples and added 5 g (⅛ oz) of champagne yeast, but different brands of yeast will have different usage recommendations, so please follow those. And please don't use bread-making yeast here — they're two completely different things! We bought our champagne yeast from a brewing shop.

Run the apples through a juicer — no need to remove the skins or cores. This gives a slightly cloudier vinegar, but the sediment will settle over time.

Measure your apple juice, then pour into a large sterilised jar (see tip, page 170). Stir in the amount of yeast recommended on the packet. Cover the top of the jar with muslin (cheesecloth), held in place by a rubber band.

Leave to ferment in a cool dark place, out of direct sunlight, for 5–7 days. The actual timing will depend on the ambient room temperature, yeast culture and the amount of natural sugar in your apples.

Once it stops bubbling and starts to settle in the jar, strain the cider into another sterilised jar, leaving the yeast sediment behind. (Having some yeast sediment in the cider isn't a problem, so no need to be too thorough.) Add the vinegar mother culture to the strained apple cider. Cover the jar with a fresh piece of muslin and leave in a cool dark place, allowing the cider to transform into vinegar as the mother culture works its magic.

Taste the vinegar after about 1 month. If it's to your liking, strain the mother off and begin a new batch of vinegar. Otherwise, leave to mature until you have the flavour you're after. (If you want to keep your mother without making a new batch of vinegar straight away, simply leave it in a sealed glass jar, sitting in enough vinegar to cover it completely.) The vinegar will keep for years unopened, changing in colour and sharpness as it ages.

Mixed Citrus Marmalade

*Makes 5 × 250 ml
(9 fl oz) jars*

GLUTEN FREE

900 g (2 lb) mixed citrus
— seville oranges, navel
oranges, cumquats

950 g (2 lb 2 oz) raw
sugar

100 ml (3½ fl oz) lemon
juice

There's a rambling stone cottage down the road that we desperately wanted to buy before we bought our farmhouse. It very much falls into 'renovator's delight' territory, although many might just see it as a ruin. It hasn't been lived in for years and there are sheep all but running through the hallway, yet there's something so storybook about the idea of bringing it back to life. I sometimes stop out the front when I'm driving past, just so I can let my imagination plan out the renovation and the garden overhaul. And if it's the middle of winter and the seville oranges from the old citrus tree are falling to the ground, I may 'borrow' a few so they don't go to waste. Their flavour is worth any explaining I might have to do — that classic old-school concentration of citrus with a bitter edge that would never be enjoyed if just bitten into, but is perfect in marmalade.

When I make this marmalade, I often mix in other citrus, too, just to add an extra layer of sweetness and fragrance. I don't really like jam, but marmalade on buttered sourdough with a pot of tea is like a seasonal rite of passage in the middle of winter on our hill. I use the 'whole fruit' method, which I find easier, so if you haven't made marmalade before, this could be a great starting point. You'll be borrowing windfall oranges from paddocks before you know it.

Generously fill a large jam-making pot with water and bring to the boil over high heat. Carefully add the whole citrus fruit. Boil the citrus at a rapid simmer until tender and very soft. Don't rush this process; the smaller citrus will take about 1 hour, and the oranges about 2 hours. Remove the smaller citrus as it becomes ready, using a slotted spoon. Once all the fruit has been boiled, drain and set aside until cool enough to handle.

You'll want to catch all the fruit juice when you cut the citrus; I place a chopping board on a wire rack set over a baking dish, so any juices will run into in the baking dish underneath. Slice the fruit in halves to expose the seeds, so you can remove them. Scoop out the citrus flesh as best as you can and roughly chop it. Slice the peel into thin strips.

Return the peel and chopped fruit to your jam-making pan. Add the sugar and lemon juice and stir to combine, using a long-handled wooden spoon to avoid very hot marmalade splatters. Bring to the boil, stirring constantly, until the temperature reaches just over 100ºC (210ºF). If you don't have a thermometer, use the 'plate' test by dropping a little bit of marmalade onto a cool plate. If the marmalade sets, it's ready; if not, cook a little longer and keep testing.

Take the marmalade off the heat and let it sit for 2–3 minutes. Give it a stir to evenly disperse the fruit, then ladle the hot marmalade into warm sterilised jars (see tip, page 170) and seal immediately.

Leave the jars undisturbed on your bench for at least 24 hours; your marmalade will then be ready to eat. It will keep, unopened, in a cool dark place for at least 6 months. Once opened, store in the fridge and use within 3 months.

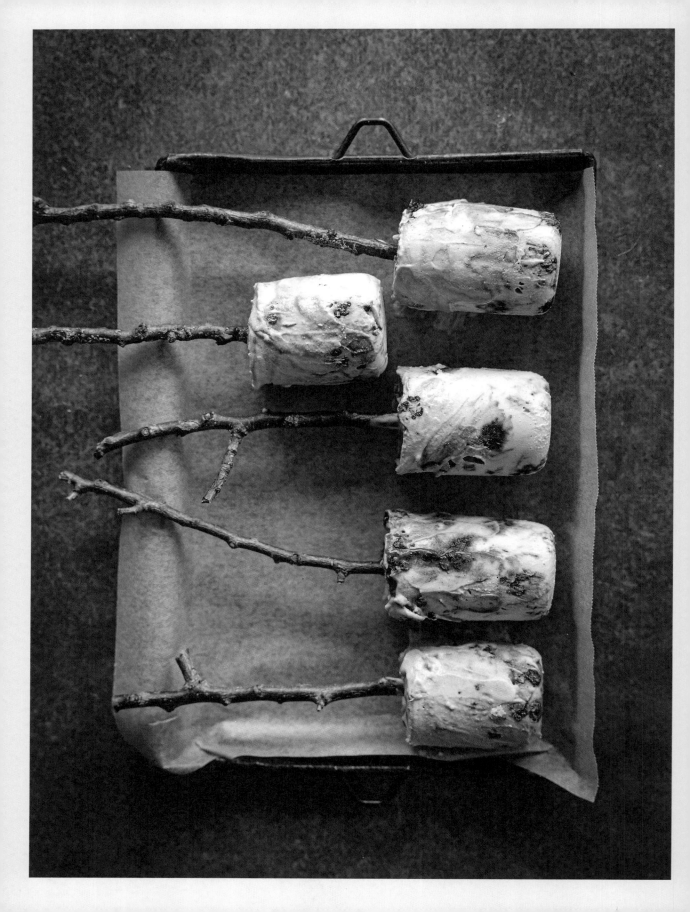

Mulberry Ice Cream on Sticks

Makes 6

200 g (7 oz) mulberries

6 x 15 cm (6 in) grapevine or fruit tree branch cuttings, or wooden ice cream sticks

300 g (10½ oz) dairy-free chocolate drops

ICE CREAM BASE

190 g (6½ oz) cashews, soaked overnight in water

400 ml (14 fl oz) coconut cream

40 g (1½ oz) rapadura sugar

80 g (2¾ oz) maple syrup

8 g (2 teaspoons) vanilla bean paste

20 g (¾ oz) coconut oil, solid not melted

Mulberries are made for foraging. Their incomparable flavour is one thing, but there's also the practical fact that mulberries can only be picked ripe — and that's when they are most fragile, so it's virtually impossible to package them up and freight them without having mulberry jam at their destination.

I'd never had mulberries until we came back to the Barossa to visit friends who were housesitting a farm that happened to have a mulberry tree laden with fruit that they needed help to pick. After being shown how to 'tickle' them from the tree, I ate one mulberry for every mulberry that made it into our little bucket. They were still warm from the sun, juice ran everywhere as we picked them, and I was absolutely smitten with the whole messy, delicious process.

We made ice cream that night after dinner and vowed to plant a mulberry tree if ever we had space beyond our inner Sydney apartment courtyard. Many years later we do have a beautiful little mulberry tree that gives us just enough fruit for dessert in summer, but I still welcome any chance to 'help' friends get through their mulberry harvest. Mulberries freeze really well for a clafoutis or a cake at a later stage — and choc-dipping them is only ever a good thing, too.

As with my other ice cream recipe on page 84, this is best made with an ice cream machine. You will need to soak the cashews the night before.

To make the ice cream base, start by soaking the cashews overnight in water.

Next day, drain the cashews and place in a high-speed blender with the coconut cream, sugar, maple syrup and vanilla paste. Blitz until very smooth. Add the coconut oil and blitz again to emulsify, but without heating the oil too much, so the mixture doesn't split. Pour into your ice cream machine and follow the manufacturer's churning instructions.

Once the ice cream has been churned but is still soft, gently stir the mulberries through, being careful not to break them up too much. Pour into six ice cream moulds or small cups and press a vine cutting or wooden stick into the centre of each, stopping before you hit the base of the mould or cup. Freeze for 2–3 hours to set, or overnight. (I've made these up to a week ahead, and left them in the freezer until just before choc-dipping them for serving.)

Melt the chocolate in a double boiler, or in a heatproof bowl set over a saucepan of simmering water. Pour the chocolate into a tall, narrow, heatproof container. Quickly dip each ice cream into the chocolate to coat all over, and place on a sheet of baking paper.

Put the ice creams back in the freezer for about 30 minutes to set the chocolate, then serve immediately. You could leave them in the freezer once you have choc-dipped them, but I find they're a little difficult to protect from being bumped around once removed from their moulds and coated in chocolate.

Dill Cucumbers with
Green Tea & Vine Leaves

*Makes a 2 litre
(70 fl oz) jar*

8–10 fresh unsprayed
vine leaves

400–600 g
(14 oz–1 lb 5 oz)
small pickling
cucumbers

3–4 dried dill heads

70 g (2½ oz) salt

1.65 litres
(57 fl oz) water, at
room temperature

15 g (½ oz) green tea
leaves

Nothing takes me back to the summers of my childhood faster than the smell of dill cucumbers. It's a bit of a thing here in the Barossa, and although the process is really very simple, it can be serious business! Our family friends always had tins of dill cucumbers lined up in their pantry, all handmade by their 'Nana-in-the-vineyard' as they called her, so as to distinguish her from their other Nana who lived in the city. I'm not sure why she did the cucumbers in old tins — probably just for the practical reason of reusing something rather than throwing it out — but I will never forget reaching my hand into that cool, murky mash of vine leaves and salt water on a stinking-hot day to feel around for a cucumber, pulling it out of the tin and eating it like a banana, without any need to cut it up, let alone worry about the juice running down my arm. That sums up summer in the Barossa for me.

Years later, I've enjoyed the nostalgia of making my own dill cucumbers — even being brave enough to ask my dad's opinion on them! — but I couldn't help tweaking the recipe just a bit. I love the idea of tea in anything, and in this case adding green tea leaves really brightens the flavour, while still allowing the dill to be the dominant taste.

Your choice if you pull the cucumbers out with a fork, or your bare hands.

Make sure your jar has been sterilised (see tip, page 170), then begin the layering process by placing a few vine leaves in the base of the jar. Add a layer of cucumbers, packing them in firmly, then add a dried dill head, squashing the seeds to release them as you go. Add another couple of vine leaves, then more cucumbers and dill.

Continue until you have filled the jar to about 2–3 cm (¾–1¼ in) from the top.

Stir the salt into the room-temperature water until dissolved. Add the green tea leaves to the top of the jar, then pour the brine over the cucumbers to fill the jar completely. Add a final vine leaf and really tuck the cucumbers in, to ensure they can't rise above the water line.

Place the lid on the jar and leave to pickle in a dark, cool place for 10–12 days.

Once opened, keep refrigerated, always pushing the cucumbers under the water line to store them. Once opened, use within 6–8 weeks.

FARMHOUSE CAKES

Chapter Seven

So many of my cakes draw inspiration from the seasonal flowers I have in my garden or see growing on the side of the road. An amazing onion flower pops up in my vegie patch... so I need to make a cake to sit it on. Why wouldn't you plan a tea party when you see — and smell — the first roadside apple blossoms? That deserves a cake! In the Barossa, cake is not an uncommon occurrence among friends gathering for tea. Making the most of rocket (arugula) flowers or trailing pea tendrils on something sweet always encourages conversations on what might be made with the wild rosehips spotted on the drive home, or where the best olive foliage might be foraged.

It's cake designed by nature... a bit wild, and definitely never perfect, but always full of real flavour and unmistakable fragrance — exactly what you want to bake, and share, and talk about, over a pot of tea.

Carrot Cake with White Chocolate Cream Cheese Icing

Makes a three-layered 20 cm (8 in) round cake, or one 26 cm (10½ in) bundt cake

560 g (1 lb 4 oz) plain (all-purpose) white spelt flour

325 g (11½ oz) rapadura sugar

10 g (2 teaspoons) Homemade Mixed Spice (page 240)

12 g (4 teaspoons) baking powder

4 g (1 teaspoon) bicarbonate of soda (baking soda)

5 g (1 teaspoon) salt

580 g (1 lb 4½ oz) grated carrot (from about 6 carrots)

290 ml (10 fl oz) orange juice (freshly squeezed)

285 ml (10 fl oz) extra virgin olive oil

155 g (5½ oz) raisins or sultanas

110 g (3¾ oz) walnuts, chopped

Chocolate probably sits at the top of most people's favourite cake list, but if I had to award the prize for 'best all-rounder' it would absolutely go to carrot cake. I've yet to come across anyone who has really strong feelings against carrot cake — plenty of strong feelings *for* carrot cake, but not one person has ever said to me, please don't make carrot cake!

I've made this carrot cake for Mum's birthday (and Dad's birthday a month later, when he said he'd like the same cake I made for mum); as a wedding cake; as a five-year-old's first day of school cake; and many, many times as an afternoon-tea cake for my girlfriends. It was on my trestle table more times than I can count when we did the farmers' market for all those years — and I've also made it gluten free by substituting my Gluten-Free Flour Blend (page 245). It holds up beautifully if you'd like to make it a day ahead and refrigerate it before icing. I've also frozen the cakes well before an occasion and let them thaw out en route to assemble on arrival.

You get the picture: this is an honest and reliable kind of carrot cake, so if you can't decide on a cake for an occasion, this cake will happily make the decision for you. I could probably bang on about this being a 'healthier' version of cake — but cake should be enjoyed, so I hope you love this and make it for the people you adore. Time to pop the kettle on.

Place all the icing ingredients in a high-speed blender and blitz until super-smooth.

If you are making a bundt version of this cake and want an icing to drizzle across the top and let run down the sides of the cake, you can use the icing immediately after blending, so it is still warm and hasn't yet set. In that case, make your icing after the bundt cake has come out of the oven and cooled. I make the same amount of icing for a bundt as I do for a layered cake because I'd rather have too much icing than not enough. That way, it's easy to be extra generous with the drizzle on the bundt.

If making the three cake layers, pour the blended icing into a container with a lid and leave to set in the fridge for 1–2 hours, until firm but not solid. (If you'd like to prepare the icing further ahead than this, simply remove it from the fridge to sit at room temperature for an hour or so, until it is at a spreadable consistency.)

Preheat your oven to 180°C (350°F).

Prepare your cake tin/s. Line the base of three 20 cm (8 in) springform cake tins with baking paper and grease the inside of the tins with olive oil. Alternatively, oil a 26 cm (10½ in) bundt (ring) tin and lightly dust with flour.

WHITE CHOCOLATE CREAM CHEESE ICING

300 g (10½ oz) raw cashews

155 g (5½ oz) maple syrup

125 g (4½ oz) cacao butter, shaved

100 ml (3½ fl oz) water

35 g (1¼ oz) extra virgin coconut oil

20 ml (½ fl oz) lemon juice

8 g (2 teaspoons) vanilla bean paste

In a large mixing bowl, combine the flour, sugar, mixed spice, baking powder, bicarbonate of soda and salt, stirring with a wooden spoon.

In a separate bowl, mix together the grated carrot, orange juice and olive oil.

Add the carrot mixture to the dry ingredients and mix together. Finally, add the raisins and walnuts and give one last mix-through, before spooning evenly into your cake tin/s.

Bake the 20 cm (8 in) cakes for 30–35 minutes, or the bundt cake for 40–50 minutes, until a skewer inserted in the cake comes out clean.

Remove from the oven and leave in the cake tin/s to cool for 10 minutes, before turning out onto a wire rack.

Be sure the cake/s are cool before beginning the icing process, and that your icing is of a spreadable consistency.

If making a round three-layered cake, place one cake on a cake plate, bottom side facing up, to give a nice flat surface. Use a palette knife to apply the icing about 1 cm (½ in) thick over the top of the cake. Sandwich the next layer of cake on top, bottom side up. Spread with another thick layer of icing, then stack the third cake on top. Now you can begin to ice the top and outside of the cake. You can completely cover the cake with icing, or you can leave parts of the cake exposed for a more dramatic effect.

Add your choice of decoration and serve immediately.

Any leftover cake will keep in an airtight container for 2–3 days.

Quince Hummingbird Cake
with Tahini Caramel

*Makes a 26 cm
(10½ in) bundt cake,
or 6 baby bundt cakes*

375 g (13 oz) plain
(all-purpose) white
spelt flour, plus extra
for dusting

390 g (13¾ oz) rapadura
sugar

10 g (1½ teaspoons)
bicarbonate of soda
(baking soda)

7 g (1¾ teaspoons)
baking powder

5 g (1 teaspoon) salt

6 g (2 teaspoons)
ground cinnamon

480 g (1 lb 1 oz) mashed
banana (from about
3 bananas)

110 ml (3¾ fl oz) extra
virgin olive oil

180 ml (6 fl oz) quince
poaching liquid, at
room temperature

8 g (2 teaspoons) vanilla
bean paste

60 ml (2 fl oz) Apple
Cider Vinegar (page 178)

150 g (5½ oz) poached
quince, chopped into
1–2 cm (½–¾ in) pieces

75 g (2½ oz) pecans,
chopped

A surprising story accompanies this cake. I was flown to Japan by a large food company that has many bakery brands under its banner, to make this cake and three other recipes, after one of their senior executives saw my Instagram. Crazy but true. It wasn't as simple as that single step, but evolved over many emails, phone calls and even a visit from the Tokyo team to our farmhouse, where we wandered through our vegie garden drinking homemade kombucha and talking about all the different flowers and foliage I love using on my cakes.

Quite surreal to go from our garden on the hill to a commercial bakery in the middle of Tokyo. I loved every minute of it — except those minutes that were spent trying to figure out why none of my recipes were working... before we realised Australian cup measurements are different from Japanese cups! I have been an advocate of measuring ingredients by weight ever since. Especially when you have to do a presentation to 30 division heads of a company waiting to taste your cakes, it's these little measurement details that really come into play. Heck. Thank goodness for scales.

Everyone on the tasting team loved this version of the classic hummingbird cake, chosen because I knew — after testing it time and again for different occasions at home — that it would cut well and remain lovely and moist for days.

This recipe includes cooked quince. Knowing there are so many different ways to do that, I'll leave it to you to choose a favourite method. I like poaching a big batch of quinces when they're in season by simply packing them in a large pan with sugar, water and a vanilla bean, and cooking slowly for an hour or so, until they're tender all the way through and beautifully deep in colour (page 235). I cut the pieces of quince from the core once they're cooked, then freeze any leftovers for future cakes, or to serve over granola. Do keep the poaching liquid for this recipe, too.

The fragrance of a quince is something I would happily wear as a perfume, it's so intoxicating. I know you'll enjoy having that beautiful aroma filling up your kitchen as you're baking this cake.

Preheat your oven to 180°C (350°F). Grease a 26 cm (10½ in) bundt (ring) tin (or six baby bundt tins) with olive oil and lightly dust with flour.

In a large bowl, whisk together the flour, sugar, bicarbonate of soda, baking powder, salt and cinnamon to blend well.

In small bowl, whisk the banana, quince poaching liquid, olive oil and vanilla paste together to blend well, then whisk into the flour mixture until completely mixed through, with no dry pockets of flour.

Whisk in the vinegar until bubbles form. Mix in the quince pieces and pecans.

TAHINI CARAMEL

75 g (2½ oz) maple syrup

35 g (1¼ oz) tahini

35 g (1¼ oz) extra virgin
coconut oil

3 g (¾ teaspoon) vanilla
bean paste

Transfer the cake batter to the cake tin/s. Bake the baby bundt cakes for 30–35 minutes, or the large bundt cake for 40–50 minutes, until a skewer inserted into the centre comes out clean.

Remove from the oven and leave to cool in the tin/s for 10 minutes, before turning out onto a wire rack.

Meanwhile, melt all the tahini caramel ingredients in a small saucepan over low heat until completely emulsified. (I make the same amount of tahini caramel, whether I'm baking one large bundt cake or six smaller cakes.) Remove from the heat. Depending on how hot the weather is, you may need to let the caramel sit for 5–10 minutes to get the right consistency for drizzling. You want the caramel to run — but not sprint! It should be similar to runny honey.

When the cake/s are completely cool, drizzle the tahini caramel over the top to run down the sides. Decorate with flowers or foliage of your choice and serve immediately.

Any leftover cake will keep in an airtight container for 2–3 days.

Rye, Chocolate & Beetroot Cake with Chocolate Mousse Crème

Makes a 20 cm (8 in) round cake

GLUTEN FREE
(with Gluten-Free Flour Blend, page 245)

110 g (3¾ oz) beetroot, peeled and grated

110 g (3¾ oz) rapadura sugar

150 ml (5 fl oz) soy or almond milk

55 ml (1¾ fl oz) extra virgin olive oil

40 g (1½ oz) maple syrup

10 g (2 teaspoons) vanilla bean paste

125 g (4½ oz) rye flour

50 g (1¾ oz) raw unsweetened cacao powder

30 g (1 oz) almond meal

2 g (½ teaspoon) salt

2 g (½ teaspoon) baking powder

4 g (1 teaspoon) bicarbonate of soda (baking soda)

5 ml (1 teaspoon) Apple Cider Vinegar (page 178)

Wedding cakes are a favourite of mine. Not that I have a cake business, but if someone asks me to make their wedding cake, I can never say no, because I'm a hopeless romantic and absolutely love celebrating love. This particular cake has been a wedding cake for some of my favourite couples over the years. There's more than one reason it's been chosen time and again: it can be made gluten free if requested, by simply replacing the flour with my Gluten-Free Flour Blend (page 245); it works just as well as cupcakes as it does as a whole cake; it's a beautifully moist cake, so it lasts the distance of sitting on display all day... and the most obvious reason — it's chocolate!

When my sister asked me to make her wedding cake, her only request was that it be chocolate. She was the very opposite of a difficult bride, handing over all responsibility to me to figure out any other details beyond the flavour choice. I knew I'd make this cake for her. I also knew I wouldn't mention the beetroot in it. You really can't taste it, but the thought of beetroot in cake isn't everyone's idea of indulgence — even though, ironically, it's the very reason this cake tastes so decadent.

For my sister's wedding I used my White Chocolate Cream Icing, so feel free to play around with that from the Carrot Cake recipe on page 186. More often than not, I use this rich Chocolate Mousse Crème because it looks so lush and is the perfect backdrop for flowers and foliage. I usually don't mention it's made from avocado, either! The avocado gives the icing the most amazing mouthfeel, and again, the chocolate overrides the flavour in every way. Once you've made this mousse crème, you'll know what I mean. I often make it to have as a dessert with fresh berries, or just eat it on its own from the jar in the fridge.

The recipe below is for a single-layer 20 cm (8 in) cake, plus the amount of chocolate mousse crème needed to cover one single cake layer. Simply choose how many cake layers you would like, depending on the occasion, and multiply both the cake mix and the chocolate mousse crème quantity accordingly.

Preheat your oven to 180°C (350°F). Line the base of a 20 cm (8 in) springform cake tin with baking paper and grease the inside of the tin with olive oil.

Put the grated beetroot in a food processor with the sugar, milk, olive oil, maple syrup and vanilla paste. Blitz until smooth.

Add the remaining dry ingredients to the food processor and blitz again.

Pour the mixture into a bowl and use a spatula to quickly but evenly mix the vinegar through. Don't worry if you see white streaks — it's just the vinegar reacting with the bicarbonate of soda and baking powder, and it's a good thing!

CHOCOLATE MOUSSE CRÈME

2 avocados
(300 g/10½ oz)

155 g (5½ oz) maple
syrup

75 g (2½ oz) raw
unsweetened cacao
powder

8 g (2 teaspoons) vanilla
bean paste

2 g (½ teaspoon) salt

Immediately pour the batter into the cake tin and bake for 30–40 minutes, or until a skewer inserted into the centre of the cake comes out clean. Remove from the oven and leave to cool in the tin for 10 minutes, before turning out onto a wire rack.

While the cake is baking, make the chocolate mousse cream. Peel the avocados, remove the stones and scoop the flesh into a high-speed blender. Add the remaining ingredients and blitz until smooth and creamy. Leave in the fridge until you are ready to ice the cake.

When the cake is completely cool, smooth the icing over and decorate with your choice of flowers or foliage.

Any leftover cake will keep in an airtight container for 2–3 days.

Spiced Parsnip Cake with Peanut Butter Icing

Makes a three-layered 20 cm (8 in) round cake, or one 26 cm (10½ in) bundt cake

560 g (1 lb 4 oz) plain (all-purpose) white spelt flour

325 g (11½ oz) rapadura sugar

12 g (4 teaspoons) baking powder

4 g (1 teaspoon) bicarbonate of soda (baking soda)

5 g (1 teaspoon) salt

5 g (2½ teaspoons) ground cardamom

580 g (1 lb 4½ oz) parsnips, peeled and grated

15 g (½ oz) fresh ginger, peeled and finely grated

285 ml (10 fl oz) extra virgin olive oil

300 ml (10½ fl oz) soy or almond milk

155 g (5½ oz) dried pear, chopped into 1 cm (½ in) pieces

110 g (3¾ oz) macadamia nuts, chopped

Parsnip may not be the first flavour you think of when it comes to cake... but trust me, it's really good! With a generous dose of cardamom and fresh ginger, this cake is almost a next-level carrot cake. And the surprise of the peanut butter icing is that it brings out the natural nuttiness in the parsnip — and is just as good with other cakes, especially the Rye, Chocolate & Beetroot Cake on page 192.

I'm a big fan of parsnip and will happily eat it roasted in salads and soups, but it wasn't until I had some particularly misshapen homegrown specimens that I thought to put them in cake — no need for the prettiest parsnips when they're to be grated anyway. They have the same kind of sweetness as carrots and beetroot, and they're both cake ingredients in my mind!

When I shared my parsnip-growing woes with a local producer at the farmers' market, he just laughed and agreed 'parsnips are tricky until you get to know them'. I thought that was a nice way of giving me every reason to pay him for his parsnip mastery rather than continue trying to grow them at home on our limestone hill. And we have parsnip cake every winter, so no complaints here.

Especially if you choose to make it as a bundt, this cake is delicious with a dusting of icing (confectioners') sugar, for a simpler way of presenting it. I often do that, but definitely give the icing a try if you're a peanut butter fan.

Preheat your oven to 180°C (350°F).

Prepare your cake tin/s. Line the base of three 20 cm (8 in) springform cake tins with baking paper and grease the inside of the tins with olive oil. Alternatively, oil a 26 cm (10½ in) bundt (ring) tin and lightly dust with flour.

In a large mixing bowl, combine the flour, sugar, baking powder, bicarbonate of soda, salt and cardamom, stirring with a wooden spoon.

In a separate bowl, mix together the grated parsnip, ginger, olive oil and milk. Add to the dry ingredients and mix together. Finally, add the pear and macadamias and give one last mix-through before spooning into the cake tin/s.

Bake the 20 cm (8 in) cakes for 30–35 minutes, or the bundt cake for 40–50 minutes, until a skewer inserted into the centre comes out clean.

Remove from the oven and leave in the cake tin/s to cool for 10 minutes, before turning out onto a wire rack.

To make the icing, use an electric hand-held mixer or the beater attachment on a stand mixer to cream the peanut butter and coconut oil together until smooth. Add the vanilla paste and mix again. Add the icing sugar in increments, ensuring it is completely mixed through without any dry pockets.

PEANUT BUTTER ICING

210 g (7½ oz) smooth peanut butter (not chunky)

60 g (2 oz) extra virgin coconut oil, at room temperature, not melted

4 g (1 teaspoon) vanilla bean paste

240 g (8½ oz) icing (confectioners') sugar

20–40 ml (½–1¼ fl oz) soy or almond milk, if needed

Taste the icing at this stage. If you're happy with the taste and consistency, you won't need to add the soy milk. This will depend on how oily your peanut butter is. Adding the milk will thicken the icing. You will see the icing initially go crumbly after the milk is added; just keep adding the milk in increments until the icing pulls together again, so as not to make the icing too runny. If, on the other hand, you find the icing too runny even before adding the milk, you can always add more icing sugar, bit by bit, to thicken the icing.

Make sure the cake/s are completely cool before icing and decorating.

If making a round three-layered cake, place one cake on a cake plate, bottom side facing up, to give a nice flat surface. Use a palette knife to apply the icing about 5 mm to 1 cm (¼–½ in) thick over the top of the cake. Sandwich the next layer of cake on top, bottom side up. Spread with another thick layer of icing, then stack the third cake on top. Now you can begin to ice the top and outside of the cake. Dip your knife into boiling water to do a final run across the icing if you prefer a super-smooth finish; otherwise, leave it a bit rustic.

If you would like to use this icing for a bundt cake, you can simply dollop it on top of the cake in generous spoonfuls.

Decorate with your choice of edible flowers or foliage and serve immediately.

Any leftover cake will keep in an airtight container for 2–3 days.

Meyer Lemon & Almond Ricotta Cake with Meringue Icing

Makes a three-layered 20 cm (8 in) round cake

400 g (14 oz) Almond Ricotta (page 227)

245 ml (8¾ fl oz) soy or almond milk

300 g (10½ oz) rapadura sugar

140 ml (4½ fl oz) extra virgin olive oil

zest and juice of 4 Meyer lemons

450 g (1 lb) plain (all-purpose) white spelt flour

9 g (1½ teaspoons) bicarbonate of soda (baking soda)

4 g (1 teaspoon) baking powder

3 g (½ teaspoon) salt

MERINGUE ICING

240 ml (8 fl oz) chickpea liquid (aquafaba), drained from a 400 g (14 oz) tin of chickpeas

265 g (9½ oz) raw sugar (not rapadura, unless you'd like a caramel-coloured meringue)

3 g (1 teaspoon) cream of tartar

If you need a show-stopper cake for an occasion, I'm going to boldly suggest you've found it in this lemon cake. The only catch is that this isn't one of those cakes that can be made well ahead of time and still look perfect hours later. I've made the actual cake layers for this recipe and frozen them in advance, so the cake part is fine — it's the meringue that will need your last-minute attention. It will absolutely be worth your time and effort, though, because nothing says fancy in quite the same way as dollops of toasted meringue. I love watching people's faces when this cake is placed on the table amid teacups, cake plates and fresh flowers. I know you're going to love receiving that reaction as much as you'll love *eating* this pretty cake.

For those yet to jump into the world of egg-less meringue, made with aquafaba — welcome! This really is the perfect cake for using it as an icing. The Meyer lemon gives just the right amount of tang to offset the sweetness of the aquafaba, and the almond ricotta adds a gorgeous texture against the softness of the meringue. And the meringue itself really is delicious — with no hint of chickpea taste. (I still only tell people after they've devoured their first slice of cake, though, to totally seal the deal on the wow factor.)

You will need a stand mixer or hand-held electric mixer for the aquafaba; the meringue is not really something that can be made with a hand whisk.

Watching the liquid drained from a can of chickpeas turn into clouds of white meringue is quite something to behold. It's like a kitchen chemistry experiment — so much so you might find yourself making it just for that dramatic 'before and after' magical reveal.

Preheat your oven to 180°C (350°F). Line the base of three 20 cm (8 in) springform cake tins with baking paper and grease the inside of the tins with olive oil.

Using a stand mixer or hand-held electric mixer, blend the almond ricotta with the milk until smooth. Add the sugar, olive oil, lemon zest and lemon juice and mix again.

Now add the flour, bicarbonate of soda, baking powder and salt. Mix once more, until completely blended into a smooth batter.

Divide the cake batter equally between the cake tins. Bake for 35–40 minutes, or until a skewer inserted into the centre of the cakes comes out clean.

Remove from the oven and leave to cool in the tins for 10 minutes, before turning out onto a wire rack.

Once the cakes have cooled, and just before assembling and serving the cake, make the meringue icing. Aquafaba is better used closest to the time of eating. Also make sure your bowl and beaters are very clean and dry.

Pour the chickpea liquid into the bowl. Add the sugar and cream of tartar. Using the balloon whisk attachment, beat the mixture on low speed for exactly 2 minutes. This will give the sugar a chance to dissolve into the aquafaba.

Turn the setting to medium speed and continue mixing for another 2 minutes.

Finally, turn the speed all the way to high and whisk for 6 minutes. You cannot over-beat aquafaba in the same way you can egg whites, so if you leave it mixing for longer, that's fine — just don't under-mix it. The timing is really important to the success of meringue.

To assemble the cake, place one cake on a cake plate, bottom side facing up, to give a nice flat surface. Top with a generous amount of the meringue, then sandwich the next layer of cake on top, bottom side up. Repeat the process, then dollop the remaining meringue on top of the cake, and around the side if you like.

If you have a mini kitchen blowtorch, you can use it to toast the layers of meringue icing until golden. (Remember, this meringue contains no egg white, so it's perfectly safe to eat raw.) Decorate with fresh almond blossoms, or any unsprayed flowers from your garden.

Any leftover cake will keep in an airtight container for 2–3 days.

Whole Mandarin Cake with Poppy Seed Icing

*Makes a 20 cm (8 in)
round cake, or a 20 cm
(8 in) long bar cake*

80 g (2¾ oz) dried
coconut shavings

180 g (6 oz) whole
mandarins (about
2 mandarins), unpeeled

280 g (10 oz) coconut
nectar syrup

100 ml (3½ fl oz) extra
virgin olive oil

8 ml (1½ teaspoons)
Apple Cider Vinegar
(page 178)

8 g (2 teaspoons) vanilla
bean paste

3 g (½ teaspoon) salt

230 g (8½ oz) plain
(all-purpose) white
spelt flour

7 g (1¾ teaspoons)
baking powder

3 g (¾ teaspoon)
bicarbonate of soda
(baking soda)

5 g (1 teaspoon)
Homemade Mixed
Spice (page 240)

My mum makes the most delicious whole orange cake, from a recipe given to her years ago by a friend. Mum tweaked the recipe a bit, and I made a few more changes so that it could be plant-based. Don't you love how recipes weave their way through different lives and evolve with each custodian? It's one of my favourite things about cooking and growing food — discovering how everyone else does it. Mum's recipe originally used oranges, but when life hands you mandarins...

Sometimes I wonder if we'll ever get around to planting a mandarin tree when the generosity of green-thumbed friends always manages to fill the gaps in our orchard produce, in the same way I hope the fruit we have in abundance joins the dots for them each season. I'm all for the idea that we might have trees groaning with figs because they're well suited here, while at the same time one of our friends has plenty of nashi pears on their trees, a fruit that has never taken to our limestone hill. It's an easy trade and all the more precious when the offer of produce happens independently of any agenda of reciprocity. That's how we manage to end up with lots of sweet mandarins each year, and the reason this cake went through its most recent evolution.

You can make this as a multi-layered cake fit for social media, or just make one layer for a simple farmhouse teacake, because we all need a reliable afternoon tea option when we feel like catching up with friends over a pot of Earl Grey. It doesn't even need the icing if you'd rather leave it unadorned, but try it iced at least once, just so you can taste how delicious poppy seeds are on the outside of a citrus cake, rather than always mixed into the batter. I hope you make it over and over until you know it by heart.

This recipe makes one 20 cm (8 in) round cake; you can multiply the quantity, along with the icing, if you would like to stack cake layers for a fancier version. If you prefer a simple teacake, bake it in a loaf (bar) tin.

Preheat your oven to 180°C (350°F). Prepare your choice of cake tin. Line the base of a 20 cm (8 in) springform cake tin with baking paper and grease the inside of the tin with olive oil. Alternatively, grease a loaf (bar) tin, measuring 20 cm (8 in) x 8 cm (3¼ in) x 6 cm (2½ in), and lightly dust with flour.

Using a food processor, grind the dried coconut into a flour. Add the whole mandarins, along with the coconut syrup, olive oil, vinegar, vanilla paste and salt. Process until smooth.

Add the flour, baking powder, bicarbonate of soda and mixed spice and blitz until just combined.

POPPY SEED ICING

150 g (5½ oz) raw cashews

80 g (2¾ oz) coconut nectar syrup

50 g (1¾ oz) cacao butter, shaved

50 ml (1¾ fl oz) water

15 g (½ oz) extra virgin coconut oil

10 ml (2 teaspoons) lemon juice

4 g (1 teaspoon) vanilla bean paste

10 g (3 teaspoons) poppy seeds

Spoon the cake batter into your cake or loaf tin and bake for 45–50 minutes, until a skewer inserted into the centre comes out clean. Remove from the oven and leave to rest in the tin for 10 minutes, before turning the cake out to cool on a wire rack.

To make the icing, place all the ingredients, except the poppy seeds, in a high-speed blender and blitz until super smooth. (Keep the poppy seeds aside to stir through by hand once the icing has set; if you add them at this stage, they will darken the icing too much.)

Pour the icing into an airtight container and leave in the fridge to set for 1–2 hours, until firm but not solid. (If you would like to prepare the icing well ahead of time, simply remove it from the fridge to sit at room temperature for an hour or so, until it is at a spreadable consistency.)

When you are ready to ice the cake, and the cake is completely cool, add the poppy seeds to the icing and stir through by hand.

Smooth the icing over the cake and decorate with your choice of edible flowers, fresh passionfruit pulp or dried orange slices.

Any leftover cake will keep in an airtight container for 2–3 days.

SEASONAL TARTS

Chapter Eight

Dessert brings people together, and I love that, which is why I try to make cakes and tarts that can accommodate as many tastes and dietary needs as possible. Making tarts to sell at the Barossa Farmers' Market was my best crash-course in making sweets to suit all occasions and requests. Wholefood, plant-based tarts ticked so many boxes, and are exactly the kind of dessert I love making and eating, so it became something I looked forward to creating each week. I had customers (and social media followers from further afield) waiting for Friday nights when I'd share what the next day's #breakfastcake would be. Good fun. Which is what eating sweets should be.

Caramel Crème Pecan Tart with Cinnamon & Maple Crust

*Makes a 28 cm
(11¼ in) tart*

GLUTEN FREE

**CINNAMON &
MAPLE CRUST**

315 g (11 oz) raw
almonds, with skin on

3 g (1 teaspoon) ground
cinnamon

1 g (¼ teaspoon) salt

50 g (1¾ oz) maple
syrup

12 g (½ oz) extra virgin
coconut oil

**CARAMEL CRÈME
FILLING**

450 g (1 lb) raw cashews

200 g (7 oz) coconut
nectar syrup

150 ml (5 fl oz) water

100 g (3½ oz) medjool
dates, pits removed

85 ml (2¾ fl oz) lemon
juice

10 g (2 teaspoons)
vanilla bean paste

3 g (½ teaspoon) salt

100 g (3½ oz) extra
virgin coconut oil

This is the one recipe I've kept up my sleeve, waiting until I could share the process properly. Although I've made so many versions of this raw tart, it is still the kind of recipe that requires some concentration. No individual step is tricky, but everything needs to be done in a certain order and within a particular time frame. This is the reason I never scribbled it down on a brown paper bag to pass across the farmers' market trestle table as I did with other simpler recipe requests.

You will definitely need a high-speed blender for this recipe; I can't see any way around that, sorry! You'll also need a good food processor to blend the tart base ingredients, for a different texture to the filling – as well as a non-stick tart (flan) tin with a removable base to assemble the tart in.

You'll get a feel for making this and the other tarts in this chapter quite quickly, but give yourself time to get into the swing of things without rushing the process or tweaking the flavours too early on. After you've nailed the basics, you'll be free to come up with all sorts of luscious flavour combinations based on what's in season.

Another tip I can give is to freeze the filled tart for a couple of hours before taking it out to thaw just enough to cut through, then leave in the fridge to serve as pre-cut slices. If you'd rather just refrigerate the tart, that's absolutely an option, but you may not get that perfect edge to the cut slices. I promise it will taste indulgent either way.

Cut a circle of baking paper to fit exactly in the base of a 28 cm (11¼ in) fluted, non-stick tart (flan) tin with a removable base. I trace around the tart base with a pencil onto a sheet of baking paper, then cut the circle out with scissors. Line the base of the tin with the baking paper, so you can slide the tart onto a serving plate more easily when you're ready to eat it.

To make the crust, place the almonds, cinnamon and salt in a food processor and blitz until the mixture resembles almond meal. You still want some texture, not almond butter! Add the maple syrup and coconut oil and blitz again. You want to make sure the crust is evenly mixed, but not overly processed, or it won't come out of the tin later on. To test whether it has the right consistency, squeeze some of the mixture between your thumb and forefinger — if it just holds together, it's ready. If the mixture falls apart after squeezing it, give it another quick blitz and test it again.

Place the crust mixture in the tart tin and, using the flats of your hands, gently even the mixture out with the top of the tart tin. It won't be compressed at this stage; this step just makes it easier to get an even thickness in the crust once you start pressing it into the tin. Using your thumb and forefinger, work your way around the side of the tart tin, pulling the mixture towards the side

200–250 g (7–9 oz)
whole pecans

with your forefinger and compressing it by having your thumb exactly opposite your forefinger, but on the outside of the tart tin. Your thumb will help keep the crust in alignment with the edge of the tart tin as well — almost as though you'd already trimmed the edges if you were making a pastry base. You should end up with a compressed crust up the side of the tin, about 5–8 mm (¼–⅜ in) thick. Be firm in pushing the crust into the flutes of the tin, so the sides of your tart don't collapse when you remove it from the tin.

Once the sides have been compressed, spread the remaining crust mixture evenly across the base, using the flat part of your fingertips to press the bottom of the crust evenly across the base. Make sure you compress the crust into the 'corner edge' of the tart tin, all the way around the base.

Place the tart tin, complete with compressed crust, in the freezer while you make the filling.

To make the filling, place the cashews, coconut syrup, water, dates, lemon juice, vanilla paste and salt in a high-speed blender. (Leave the coconut oil out at this stage, otherwise it will split with the heat of the motor.) Blitz until very smooth; this will take 4–6 minutes, depending on your blender. I have an agitator with my Vitamix and use it to constantly push the cashew mixture down the sides of the blender. You might need to stop your machine a few times to do this with a spatula if you don't have a purpose-made agitator.

Once the mixture is very smooth, with the consistency of tahini, add the coconut oil and give a final blitz to emulsify the mixture. Don't over-mix at this stage — it should only take 30 seconds to 1 minute to completely 'dissolve' the coconut oil into the filling.

Remove the tart tin from the freezer. Pour in the filling, smoothing it out with a spatula, making sure there's no trapped air bubbles. Decorate with the pecans.

Refrigerate or freeze. If you freeze the tart for a few hours, then thaw it just enough to be able to cut it into slices, it will give a cleaner edge to the slices.

Any leftover tart can be sealed in plastic wrap and stashed in the freezer for at least a month, for a sneaky dessert when the moment arises. I'm actually happy eating a piece of raw tart while it's frozen, and many of my friends feel the same. It will only take 15–20 minutes to thaw, depending on the ambient temperature in your kitchen.

Blood Plum, Cacao & Black Tahini Tart with Dark Chocolate Crust

Makes a 28 cm (11¼ in) tart

GLUTEN FREE

DARK CHOCOLATE CRUST

260 g (9¼ oz) raw almonds, with skin on

30 g (1 oz) cacao nibs

25 g (1 oz) raw unsweetened cacao powder

1 g (¼ teaspoon) salt

50 g (1¾ oz) coconut nectar syrup

15 g (½ oz) extra virgin coconut oil

This is one of my favourite tarts because of the drama that black tahini and dark chocolate introduce to the already rich colour of blood plums. It also gives the opportunity to play around with stone fruit as the decoration on top. You can swap the blood plums for any other stone fruit that happens to be in season to make this recipe more your own creation. I love the aesthetics of perfectly placed concentric circles of fruit — it's such a stunning pay-off for very little effort... and I know you'll be doing peach and nectarine tarts before too long as well.

If you're not a lover of tahini, I'm still going to encourage you try this tart, because it's more about the black tahini bringing out the flavour of the chocolate in the raw cacao, rather than being focused on as an individual ingredient. My mum isn't a huge fan of any kind of tahini, but she absolutely loved this combination, so I feel confident it will land happily on your table.

The heady fragrance of the blood plums cannot be overstated, either — it's the smell of autumn to me. Do wait for the plums to be really ripe before making this tart; their perfume will tell you when they are.

Cut a circle of baking paper to fit exactly in the base of a 28 cm (11¼ in) fluted, non-stick tart (flan) tin with a removable base. I trace around the tart base with a pencil onto a sheet of baking paper, then cut the circle out with scissors. Line the base of the tin with the baking paper, so you can slide the tart onto a serving plate more easily when you're ready to eat it.

To make the crust, place the almonds, cacao nibs, cacao powder and salt in a food processor and blitz until the mixture resembles almond meal. You still want some texture, not almond butter! Add the coconut syrup and coconut oil and blitz again. You want to make sure the crust is evenly mixed, but not overly processed, or it won't come out of the tin later on. To test whether it has the right consistency, squeeze some of the mixture between your thumb and forefinger — if it just holds together, it's ready. If the mixture falls apart after squeezing it, give it another quick blitz and test it again.

Place the crust mixture in the tart tin and, using the flats of your hands, gently even the mixture out with the top of the tart tin. It won't be compressed at this stage; this step just makes it easier to get an even thickness in the crust once you start pressing it into the tin. Using your thumb and forefinger, work your way around the side of the tart tin, pulling the mixture towards the side with your forefinger and compressing it by having your thumb exactly opposite your forefinger, but on the outside of the tart tin. Your thumb will help keep the crust in alignment with the edge of the tart tin as well — almost as though you'd

CACAO & BLACK TAHINI FILLING

460 g (1 lb) raw cashews

200 g (7 oz) coconut nectar syrup

180 ml (6 fl oz) water

60 g (2 oz) raw unsweetened cacao powder

40 g (1½ oz) black tahini

15 g (½ oz) vanilla bean paste

3 g (½ teaspoon) salt

100 g (3½ oz) extra virgin coconut oil

TOPPING

400 g (14 oz) blood plums (about 6 plums)

dark rose petals or edible flowers (optional)

already trimmed the edges if you were making a pastry base. You should end up with a compressed crust up the side of the tin, about 5–8 mm (¼–⅜ in) thick. Be firm in pushing the crust into the flutes of the tin, so the sides of your tart don't collapse when you remove it from the tin.

Once the sides have been compressed, spread the remaining crust mixture evenly across the base, using the flat part of your fingertips to press the bottom of the crust evenly across the base. Make sure you compress the crust into the 'corner edge' of the tart tin, all the way around the base.

Place the tart tin, complete with compressed crust, in the freezer while you make the filling.

To make the filling, place the cashews, coconut syrup, water, cacao powder, tahini, vanilla paste and salt in a high-speed blender. (Leave the coconut oil out at this stage, otherwise it will split with the heat of the motor.) Blitz until very smooth; this will take 4–6 minutes, depending on your blender. I have an agitator with my Vitamix and use it to constantly push the cashew mixture down the sides of the blender. You might need to stop your machine a few times to do this with a spatula if you don't have a purpose-made agitator.

Once the mixture is very smooth, with the consistency of tahini, add the coconut oil and give a final blitz to emulsify the mixture. Don't over-mix at this stage — it should only take 30 seconds to 1 minute to completely 'dissolve' the coconut oil into the filling.

Remove the tart tin from the freezer. Pour in the filling, smoothing it out with a spatula, making sure there are no trapped air bubbles.

To decorate, cut each plum into 12 segments and remove the stones. Place a segment of plum slightly overlapping the next in a concentric circle around the outer edge of the tart. Add another circle of plum segments inside the first circle, then finish with three or four plum segments in the centre of the tart. Decorate with flowers or petals if using.

Refrigerate or freeze. If you freeze the tart for a few hours, then thaw it just enough to be able to cut it into slices, it will give a cleaner edge to the slices.

Any leftover tart can be sealed in plastic wrap and stashed in the freezer for at least a month. It will only take 15–20 minutes to thaw, depending on the ambient temperature in your kitchen.

Lemon Verbena Tart with Macadamia & Lemon Zest Crust

*Makes a 28 cm
(11¼ in) tart*

GLUTEN FREE

**MACADAMIA &
LEMON ZEST CRUST**

200 g (7 oz) raw
almonds, with skin on

zest of 2 lemons

1 g (¼ teaspoon) salt

115 g (4 oz) macadamias

50 g (1¾ oz) coconut
nectar syrup

12 g (½ oz) extra virgin
coconut oil

A classic lemon tart is always a good bet, because there aren't too many people who don't like that bright and delicious combination of citrus in a sweet, creamy base. This isn't exactly a classic lemon tart in that it's gluten free, plant-based and raw, but it still ticks all the same boxes. The lemon verbena gives the opportunity to include tea in a recipe once again — and I'm all for that!

I use Meyer lemons for this tart whenever they're in season, but I don't really move the ingredients around a lot with this recipe. You can decorate the top with whatever fruit or flowers take your fancy — or simply leave it unadorned. I love the option of simply adding some fresh lemon verbena from the garden, especially when it's in flower, and letting the lemon be the star of the show.

It's probably worth noting that the less decoration on top of the tart, the easier it will be to cut, so this tart might be a good starting point to get a feel for how each component comes together, and whether you'd prefer to refrigerate or freeze before cutting and serving — and add any decorations once you're more familiar with each step.

Cut a circle of baking paper to fit exactly in the base of a 28 cm (11¼ in) fluted, non-stick tart (flan) tin with a removable base. I trace around the tart base with a pencil onto a sheet of baking paper, then cut the circle out with scissors. Line the base of the tin with the baking paper, so you can slide the tart onto a serving plate more easily when you're ready to eat it.

To make the crust, place the almonds, lemon zest and salt in a food processor and blitz until the mixture resembles almond meal. You still want some texture, not almond butter! Add the macadamias and blitz again. (Don't add the macadamias at the same time as the almonds, because the almonds take longer to process into a fine meal — and by that stage, the softer macadamias would be a purée.) Now add the coconut syrup and coconut oil and blitz again. You want to make sure the crust is evenly mixed, but not overly processed, or it won't come out of the tin later on. To test whether it has the right consistency, squeeze some of the mixture between your thumb and forefinger — if it just holds together, it's ready. If the mixture falls apart after squeezing it, give it another quick blitz and test it again.

Place the crust mixture in the tart tin and, using the flats of your hands, gently even the mixture out with the top of the tart tin. It won't be compressed at this stage; this step just makes it easier to get an even thickness in the crust once you start pressing it into the tin. Using your thumb and forefinger, work your way around the side of the tart tin, pulling the mixture towards the side with your forefinger and compressing it by having your thumb exactly opposite your forefinger, but on the outside of the tart tin. Your thumb will help keep the crust in alignment with the edge of the tart tin as well — almost as though you'd

LEMON VERBENA FILLING

450 g (1 lb) raw cashews

200 g (7 oz) coconut nectar syrup

150 ml (5 fl oz) lemon verbena tea, cooled

zest of 2 lemons

85 ml (2¾ fl oz) lemon juice

10 g (2 teaspoons) vanilla bean paste

3 g (½ teaspoon) salt

1 g (¼ teaspoon) ground turmeric

100 g (3½ oz) extra virgin coconut oil

TOPPING

fresh unsprayed lemon verbena leaves, or other foliage and flowers

already trimmed the edges if you were making a pastry base. You should end up with a compressed crust up the side of the tin, about 5–8 mm (¼–⅜ in) thick. Be firm in pushing the crust into the flutes of the tin, so the sides of your tart don't collapse when you remove it from the tin.

Once the sides have been compressed, spread the remaining crust mixture evenly across the base, using the flat part of your fingertips to press the bottom of the crust evenly across the base. Make sure you compress the crust into the 'corner edge' of the tart tin, all the way around the base.

To make the filling, place the cashews, coconut syrup, tea, lemon zest, lemon juice, vanilla paste, salt and turmeric in a high-speed blender. (Leave the coconut oil out at this stage, otherwise it will split with the heat of the motor.) Blitz until very smooth; this will take 4–6 minutes, depending on your blender. I have an agitator with my Vitamix and use it to constantly push the cashew mixture down the sides of the blender. You might need to stop your machine a few times to do this with a spatula if you don't have a purpose-made agitator.

Once the mixture is very smooth, with the consistency of tahini, add the coconut oil and give a final blitz to emulsify the mixture. Don't over-mix at this stage — it should only take 30 seconds to 1 minute to completely 'dissolve' the coconut oil into the filling.

Remove the tart tin from the freezer. Pour in the filling, smoothing it out with a spatula, making sure there are no trapped air bubbles.

Refrigerate or freeze. If you freeze the tart for a few hours, then thaw it just enough to be able to cut it into slices, it will give a cleaner edge to the slices. Decorate with the lemon verbena leaves just before serving, so they remain nice and fresh.

Any leftover tart can be sealed in plastic wrap and stashed in the freezer for at least a month. It will only take 15–20 minutes to thaw, depending on the ambient temperature in your kitchen.

White Chocolate, Fig & Pistachio Tart with Cardamom Crust

*Makes a 28 cm
(11¼ in) tart*

GLUTEN FREE

CARDAMOM CRUST

315 g (11 oz) raw
almonds, with skin on

5 g (2½ teaspoons)
freshly ground
cardamom

1 g (¼ teaspoon) salt

50 g (1¾ oz) maple
syrup

12 g (½ oz) extra virgin
coconut oil

WHITE CHOCOLATE
FILLING

450 g (1 lb) raw cashews

200 g (7 oz) coconut
nectar syrup

150 ml (5 fl oz) water

85 ml (2¾ fl oz) lemon
juice

70 g (2½ oz) cacao
butter, shaved

10 g (2 teaspoons)
vanilla bean paste

3 g (½ teaspoon) salt

100 g (3½ oz) extra
virgin coconut oil

Cacao butter adds the most extraordinary creaminess to this tart. In fact, it adds an unmistakable mouthfeel to anything it is added to, so try some in your smoothies or hot chocolate for an indulgent upgrade! I love using it in cake icing for the luxury it adds, but it's also beautiful in this tart because it has all the flavour of white chocolate, without any need for dairy. It melts at body temperature, so if you happen to drop some in the kitchen, just use it as a moisturiser on your hands rather than waste it. Or, purposely break a chunk off to massage into your skin after your next bath. I love the stuff.

You can buy cacao butter in buttons, like choc-drops, or in a block that can easily be shaved, as it is quite soft even when it's solid. I usually buy it in blocks, because I tend to use quite a bit of it in my cooking, and I find the shavings easier to work with. Either form will work for this recipe, because it will be blitzed in a high-speed blender.

This is probably the tart filling I make the most, as it's such a great base for so many fruit options. If figs aren't available, fresh raspberries, cherries, blackberries or strawberries all fit the bill perfectly.

Cut a circle of baking paper to fit exactly in the base of a 28 cm (11¼ in) fluted, non-stick tart (flan) tin with a removable base. I trace around the tart base with a pencil onto a sheet of baking paper, then cut the circle out with scissors. Line the base of the tin with the baking paper, so you can slide the tart onto a serving plate more easily when you're ready to eat it.

To make the crust, place the almonds, cardamom and salt in a food processor and blitz until the mixture resembles almond meal. You still want some texture, not almond butter! Add the maple syrup and coconut oil and blitz again. You want to make sure the crust is evenly mixed, but not overly processed, or it won't come out of the tin later on. To test whether it has the right consistency, squeeze some of the mixture between your thumb and forefinger — if it just holds together, it's ready. If the mixture falls apart after squeezing it, give it another quick blitz and test it again.

Place the crust mixture in the tart tin and, using the flats of your hands, gently even the mixture out with the top of the tart tin. It won't be compressed at this stage; this step just makes it easier to get an even thickness in the crust once you start pressing it into the tin. Using your thumb and forefinger, work your way around the side of the tart tin, pulling the mixture towards the side with your forefinger and compressing it by having your thumb exactly opposite your forefinger, but on the outside of the tart tin. Your thumb will help keep the crust in alignment with the edge of the tart tin as well — almost as though you'd already trimmed the edges if you were making a pastry base. You should

TOPPING

200–250 g (7–9 oz) fresh figs, sliced

75 g (2½ oz) raw pistachios, roughly chopped

end up with a compressed crust up the side of the tin, about 5–8 mm (¼–⅜ in) thick. Be firm in pushing the crust into the flutes of the tin, so the sides of your tart don't collapse when you remove it from the tin.

Once the sides have been compressed, spread the remaining crust mixture evenly across the base, using the flat part of your fingertips to press the bottom of the crust evenly across the base. Make sure you compress the crust into the 'corner edge' of the tart tin, all the way around the base.

Place the tart tin, complete with compressed crust, in the freezer while you make the filling.

To make the filling, place the cashews, coconut syrup, water, lemon juice, cacao butter, vanilla paste and salt in a high-speed blender. (Leave the coconut oil out at this stage, otherwise it will split with the heat of the motor.) Blitz until very smooth; this will take 4–6 minutes, depending on your blender. I have an agitator with my Vitamix and use it to constantly push the cashew mixture down the sides of the blender. You might need to stop your machine a few times to do this with a spatula if you don't have a purpose-made agitator.

Once the mixture is very smooth, with the consistency of tahini, add the coconut oil and give a final blitz to emulsify the mixture. Don't over-mix at this stage – it should only take 30 seconds to 1 minute to completely 'dissolve' the coconut oil into the filling.

Remove the tart tin from the freezer. Pour in the filling, smoothing it out with a spatula, making sure there are no trapped air bubbles. Decorate with the fig slices and pistachios.

Refrigerate or freeze. If you freeze the tart for a few hours, then thaw it just enough to be able to cut it into slices, it will give a cleaner edge to the slices.

Any leftover tart can be sealed in plastic wrap and stashed in the freezer for at least a month. It will only take 15–20 minutes to thaw, depending on the ambient temperature in your kitchen.

Apricot & Chamomile Crème Tart with a Pepita Crust

*Makes a 28 cm
(11¼ in) tart*

GLUTEN FREE

PEPITA CRUST

315 g (11 oz) raw
almonds, with skin on

20 g (¾ oz) pepitas
(pumpkin seeds)

1 g (¼ teaspoon) salt

50 g (1¾ oz) coconut
nectar syrup

12 g (½ oz) extra virgin
coconut oil

When we bought our farmhouse, there was an old apricot tree on the property, and although it looked a little worse for wear after years of neglect, it rewarded our efforts three-fold after we started watering it and gave it a decent pruning. We've had so many apricots from that one tree, and have since planted more apricot trees after seeing how well suited they are to our place here.

Anyone who has a fruit tree will know that, along with the fruit you manage to pick before the birds get to it, or the freak hailstorm happens, or strong winds batter the still-forming produce, you always end up with a percentage of your harvest that is less than presentable — still absolutely full of flavour, but just not the fruit you'd choose to enter in the local show. In my kitchen, those apricots usually end up in smoothies or jams, but after I had experimented with including the fruit in this tart filling, it become a favourite way to use our flavoursome 'seconds'.

You can swap the apricots for whatever stone fruit you have on hand, but definitely try the combination of apricots with chamomile first, because they make such a delicately perfumed team, as well as offering the softest colour palette. So pretty.

Cut a circle of baking paper to fit exactly in the base of a 28 cm (11¼ in) fluted, non-stick tart (flan) tin with a removable base. I trace around the tart base with a pencil onto a sheet of baking paper, then cut the circle out with scissors. Line the base of the tin with the baking paper, so you can slide the tart onto a serving plate more easily when you're ready to eat it.

To make the crust, place the almonds, pepitas and salt in a food processor and blitz until the mixture resembles almond meal. You still want some texture, not almond butter! Add the coconut syrup and coconut oil and blitz again. You want to make sure the crust is evenly mixed, but not overly processed, or it won't come out of the tin later on. To test whether it has the right consistency, squeeze some of the mixture between your thumb and forefinger — if it just holds together, it's ready. If the mixture falls apart after squeezing it, give it another quick blitz and test it again.

Place the crust mixture in the tart tin and, using the flats of your hands, gently even the mixture out with the top of the tart tin. It won't be compressed at this stage; this step just makes it easier to get an even thickness in the crust once you start pressing it into the tin. Using your thumb and forefinger, work your way around the side of the tart tin, pulling the mixture towards the side with your forefinger and compressing it by having your thumb exactly opposite your forefinger, but on the outside of the tart tin. Your thumb will help keep the crust in alignment with the edge of the tart tin as well — almost as though you'd already trimmed the edges if you were making a pastry base. You should end

APRICOT & CHAMOMILE CRÈME FILLING

450 g (1 lb) raw cashews

200 g (7 oz) fresh apricots (about 4 apricots), stones removed

200 g (7 oz) coconut nectar syrup

120 ml (4 fl oz) chamomile tea, cooled

15 ml (½ fl oz) lemon juice

10 g (2 teaspoons) vanilla bean paste

3 g (½ teaspoon) salt

100 g (3½ oz) extra virgin coconut oil

TOPPING

200–250 g (7–9 oz) fresh apricots, stones removed, flesh sliced

pepitas (pumpkin seeds)

fresh unsprayed chamomile flowers

up with a compressed crust up the side of the tin, about 5–8 mm (¼–⅜ in) thick. Be firm in pushing the crust into the flutes of the tin, so the sides of your tart don't collapse when you remove it from the tin.

Once the sides have been compressed, spread the remaining crust mixture evenly across the base, using the flat part of your fingertips to press the bottom of the crust evenly across the base. Make sure you compress the crust into the 'corner edge' of the tart tin, all the way around the base.

Place the tart tin, complete with compressed crust, in the freezer while you make the filling.

To make the filling, place the cashews, apricots, coconut syrup, chamomile tea, lemon juice, vanilla paste and salt in a high-speed blender. (Leave the coconut oil out at this stage, otherwise it will split with the heat of the motor.) Blitz until very smooth; this will take 4–6 minutes, depending on your blender. I have an agitator with my Vitamix and use it to constantly push the cashew mixture down the sides of the blender. You might need to stop your machine a few times to do this with a spatula if you don't have a purpose-made agitator.

Once the mixture is very smooth, with the consistency of tahini, add the coconut oil and give a final blitz to emulsify the mixture. Don't over-mix at this stage — it should only take 30 seconds to 1 minute to completely 'dissolve' the coconut oil into the filling.

Remove the tart tin from the freezer. Pour in the filling, smoothing it out with a spatula, making sure there are no trapped air bubbles. Decorate with the apricot slices, pepitas and chamomile flowers, or your choice of topping.

Refrigerate or freeze. If you freeze the tart for a few hours, then thaw it just enough to be able to cut it into slices, it will give a cleaner edge to the slices.

Any leftover tart can be sealed in plastic wrap and stashed in the freezer for at least a month. It will only take 15–20 minutes to thaw, depending on the ambient temperature in your kitchen.

Raspberry & Vanilla Crème Tart with Rose Spiced Crust

Makes a 28 cm (11¼ in) tart

GLUTEN FREE

ROSE SPICED CRUST

315 g (11 oz) raw almonds, with skin on

5 g (1 teaspoon) Homemade Mixed Spice (page 240)

4 g (6 teaspoons) dried rose petals

1 g (¼ teaspoon) salt

50 g (1¾ oz) maple syrup

12 g (½ oz) extra virgin coconut oil

VANILLA CRÈME FILLING

450 g (1 lb) raw cashews

200 g (7 oz) coconut nectar syrup

150 ml (5 fl oz) water

85 ml (2¾ fl oz) lemon juice

20 g (¾ oz) vanilla bean paste

3 g (½ teaspoon) salt

100 g (3½ oz) extra virgin coconut oil

A fellow gardener and dear friend gave me a few raspberry canes as I walked to my car after having tea with her one morning. I just love how naturally things like, 'Oh, would you like to try any raspberries in your glasshouse?' are said, when you're walking through someone's garden as you leave their house, already laden with fresh raspberries and a few zucchini (courgettes). The reason you'd move to the country right there.

I'm pleased to say those two little raspberry canes have loved living in our glasshouse and we've been picking raspberries from them each season. We're not yet at the stage of having so many raspberries we don't know what to do with them all, but I hope that will be the case one day. Our border collie would need to stop eating the low-hanging fruit before then, I'd imagine. He's very good at varying his diet with foraging. Fresh, ripe, homegrown raspberries, though — who can blame him?

I love adding fresh raspberries to desserts; they have a way of making anything sweet feel like you've just bought it from a glass cabinet in a fancy Parisian bakery. Of course I'm going to suggest sourcing local raspberries, in season, for this tart, but if you can't wait, thawed frozen raspberries are a perfectly acceptable substitute.

The rose spiced crust is one of my favourites. I've used it with apricots, cherries and even dark chocolate, if you'd like to do some mixing and matching once you have the hang of this one.

Cut a circle of baking paper to fit exactly in the base of a 28 cm (11¼ in) fluted, non-stick tart (flan) tin with a removable base. I trace around the tart base with a pencil onto a sheet of baking paper, then cut the circle out with scissors. Line the base of the tin with the baking paper, so you can slide the tart onto a serving plate more easily when you're ready to eat it.

To make the crust, place the almonds, mixed spice, petals and salt in a food processor and blitz until the mixture resembles almond meal. You still want some texture, not almond butter! Add the maple syrup and coconut oil and blitz again. You want to make sure the crust is evenly mixed, but not overly processed, or it won't come out of the tin later on. To test whether it has the right consistency, squeeze some of the mixture between your thumb and forefinger — if it just holds together, it's ready. If the mixture falls apart after squeezing it, give it another quick blitz and test it again.

Place the crust mixture in the tart tin and, using the flats of your hands, gently even the mixture out with the top of the tart tin. It won't be compressed at this stage; this step just makes it easier to get an even thickness in the crust once you start pressing it into the tin. Using your thumb and forefinger, work your way around the side of the tart tin, pulling the mixture towards the side

100–150 g (3½–5½ oz)
fresh raspberries

75 g (2½ oz) raw
pistachios, roughly
chopped

dried rose petals

with your forefinger and compressing it by having your thumb exactly opposite your forefinger, but on the outside of the tart tin. Your thumb will help keep the crust in alignment with the edge of the tart tin as well — almost as though you'd already trimmed the edges if you were making a pastry base. You should end up with a compressed crust up the side of the tin, about 5–8 mm (¼–⅜ in) thick. Be firm in pushing the crust into the flutes of the tin, so the sides of your tart don't collapse when you remove it from the tin.

Once the sides have been compressed, spread the remaining crust mixture evenly across the base, using the flat part of your fingertips to press the bottom of the crust evenly across the base. Make sure you compress the crust into the 'corner edge' of the tart tin, all the way around the base.

Place the tart tin, complete with compressed crust, in the freezer while you make the filling.

To make the filling, place the cashews, coconut syrup, water, lemon juice, vanilla paste and salt in a high-speed blender. (Leave the coconut oil out at this stage, otherwise it will split with the heat of the motor.) Blitz until very smooth; this will take 4–6 minutes, depending on your blender. I have an agitator with my Vitamix and use it to constantly push the cashew mixture down the sides of the blender. You might need to stop your machine a few times to do this with a spatula if you don't have a purpose-made agitator.

Once the mixture is very smooth, with a consistency of tahini, add the coconut oil and give a final blitz to emulsify it into the filling mixture. Don't over-mix at this stage — it should only take 30 seconds to 1 minute to completely dissolve the coconut oil into the filling.

Remove the tart tin from the freezer. Pour in the filling, smoothing it out with a spatula, making sure there's no trapped air bubbles. Decorate with the raspberries, pistachios and dried rose petals.

Refrigerate or freeze. If you freeze the tart for a few hours, then thaw it just enough to be able to cut it into slices, it will give a cleaner edge to the slices.

Any leftover tart can be sealed in plastic wrap and stashed in the freezer for at least a month. It will only take 15–20 minutes to thaw, depending on the ambient temperature in your kitchen.

STAPLE PROVISIONS

Chapter Nine

I love fancy recipes just as much as the next person, but
for most of the everyday meals in our kitchen, things
are kept as user-friendly as possible. That means a little
organisation, not for hours at a time or all at once, but more
as a regular cycle of a few things being made each week, or
on the weekend. I really rely on homemade versions of 'fast
food' during the week, so having a choice of foundational
flavours in jars makes every difference. Things like fresh
stock, butter and miso paste last for ages in the fridge,
so they only need to be made every month or so, while
almond ricotta and tofu are a weekly ritual — and in order
to have the nutritional hit of a green smoothie for breakfast
every day, I make a big batch about twice a week. The idea
of adding in the good stuff rather than focusing on what
'shouldn't be eaten' is so much easier when you have lentils
sprouting on the bench, and a plethora of seeds and spices
to sprinkle over everything with gomasio and seasonal
masalas. It could be argued that chocolate-dipped fennel
flowers aren't exactly a staple, but I beg to differ.

Everyday Green Smoothie

*Makes about 2 litres
(8 cups) of green smoothie
concentrate; serves 6–8*

GLUTEN FREE

950 ml (33 fl oz) water

2 large oranges, peeled

2 bananas, peeled

65 g (2½ oz) Tuscan
kale leaves; no need
to remove stems

50 g (1¾ oz) chia seeds

20 g (¾ oz) parsley
(flat-leaf or curly)

20 g (¾ oz) spirulina
powder

5 g (1 teaspoon) nettle
powder (optional)

I was a serious fresh juice devotee for years, but after jumping on the fibre bandwagon, I couldn't bear throwing all the pulp into our compost each day. Even though our ducks were pretty happy with the deal, it seemed like such a waste of good produce.

For me, this smoothie ticks all the same boxes as fresh juice, but in a way that adds a diversity of fibre to each day. I do vary this smoothie slightly, depending on seasonal extras, but the following recipe is my base across the year.

I also understand that not everyone wants to spend 20 minutes making a smoothie every morning, no matter how good it makes you feel for the rest of the day, because life is busy. Instead, I make a smoothie batch every three or four days and store it in jars in the fridge. This recipe follows that plan, making it easy to get a big hit of fibre and nutrients daily without the hassle.

I have a big glass of water when I wake up, then follow it with a glass of this green smoothie, before a cup of tea about an hour later. Caffeine interrupts the absorption of iron, and because this smoothie is loaded with all the good stuff, I just leave a bit of time between drinking my breakfast and having my first cup of tea for the day.

If you have a garden, be sure to add edible flowers like calendula or rocket (arugula), and fresh green fennel seeds or fresh green coriander seeds. Smoothies are also a great way to use up any grub-nibbled or wind-damaged leaves.

If you're super keen and make your own nettle powder by blitzing dried nettles in your food processor, you can definitely add that as well; it'll make your green smoothies really green!

Place all the ingredients in a high-speed blender and blitz until smooth. Serve immediately.

Pour the remaining mixture into glass jars and store in the fridge. The smoothie will keep for up to 5 days unopened. Once opened, consume within 3 days. I usually add some extra water on the second and third day of drinking, as the chia seeds start to thicken the smoothie.

Individual jars make a great 'traveller' option in the car, too.

Almond Ricotta

Makes about 900 g (2 lb)

GLUTEN FREE

400 g (14 oz) almonds,
no skins, soaked in cold
water overnight

220 ml (7½ fl oz) water

100 g (3½ oz) coconut
cream

8 g (2 teaspoons) salt

2 probiotic capsules
(dairy-free powder)

I'm not kidding when I say I could just about put this almond ricotta in every recipe in this book. In the same way that traditional ricotta can jump from savoury to sweet incarnations, this almond ricotta lends itself to so many different uses — so much so that if you feel a dish is missing something, just add a few dollops of this ricotta.

Fermentation — delivered via the action of the probiotics — gives this ricotta that familiar cheesy tang, so as the ricotta ages it will become stronger in flavour, and will also thicken in consistency. If you'd like to thicken it a little faster, or a little further, you can do so by hand, using muslin (cheesecloth) to wrap a cupful and squeeze it to extract the excess liquid, similar to making labneh.

I love serving this for pre-dinner nibbles with shards of thinly sliced oven-roasted sourdough and Wild Olives in Brine (page 168). To make things all the more fancy, push some ricotta into a muslin-lined cup, place a weight on top and leave in the fridge for an hour or so, before gently turning it out onto a plate and pressing fresh nasturtium leaves into the top.

After years of commercial cheesemaking, this ricotta is still the product I use the most. This recipe is adapted for home cheesemaking, but I can't emphasise enough how important it is to use clean utensils and sterilised jars. As long as you tick that box before you begin, the rest is easy.

It lasts for more than a month unopened in the fridge, provided you have very clean utensils to begin with. I usually store each batch in four jars to avoid cross-contamination once each jar is opened. It never takes us a month to eat it all, though. Not even close.

Place the almonds, water, coconut cream and salt in a high-speed blender. Carefully prise the probiotic capsules open and pour the powder into the blender. (Discard the actual capsules — you don't want those in the ricotta!) Blend until very smooth and silken, using an agitator to continually move the mixture down towards the blade, if your blender has one; this might take 3–5 minutes. Rest your blender if it gets too hot.

Scoop the blended paste into a clean, dry porcelain or glass bowl and cover with muslin (cheesecloth) to allow it to breathe. Leave at room temperature overnight to ferment.

Next morning, you should smell a lovely 'cheesy' aroma, telling you the probiotics have worked. There may even be some air bubbles in the mixture, depending on how warm the room was overnight. Taste the ricotta and, if it's to your liking, seal in sterilised jars and store in the fridge. For a stronger flavour, you can leave it for up to 4 more hours and taste again, but the total fermentation time shouldn't exceed 24 hours, or it will start getting too funky.

The ricotta is ready to use as soon as it is cold, and will continue to develop in flavour as it ages in the fridge. Use it on everything!

Clockwise from top left: Almond Ricotta (page 227), Winter Masala
(page 241), Green Miso Paste (page 233), Sprouted Almonds (page 243),
Homemade Mixed Spice (page 240), Turmeric Butter (page 230),
Bespoke Flour Mix (page 244), Wholefood Vegie Stock Paste (page 232),
Red Lentil Sprouts (page 242), Summer Masala (page 241),
Green Gomasio (page 234), Macadamia Parmesan (middle, page 231).

Turmeric Butter

*Makes about 275 g
(9½ oz)*

GLUTEN FREE

230 g (8½ oz) coconut
oil, cold from the fridge

30 ml (1 fl oz) extra
virgin olive oil, cold
from the fridge

5 g (1 teaspoon) salt

5 g (1 teaspoon)
nutritional yeast flakes

1 g (¼ teaspoon) ground
turmeric

Winter throws some of my favourite things together. Jonquils flowering under the leaf-bare apricot tree, violets beaming intense velveteen against everything green, fuzzy buds on the pear tree bunkering down until warmth comes along, and, early in the foggy mornings, spider webs glistening with enough dew to fend off runner ducks hurrying to their next appointment.

Then there's the furry new life that turns up at the coldest part of the year. Little lambs that pogo-stick around the paddocks as though the near-zero temperatures are just fine by them. And the calves. It'd be a hard heart not to be stopped in its tracks by seeing a cow give birth. Tiny hooves leading the way, superhero-style, out into the freezing cold. Determined mooing from the mumma cow as she connects into that realm where Nature seems to guide everything. Then, in a warm, slippery crash, a calf is on the ground and life cycles again. Even more amazing is how the older cows 'midwife' the younger ones who are giving birth for the first time, gathering in a circle around the birthing cow to offer support. I couldn't believe this the first time I saw it. The wisdom of the elder cows is such a beautiful thing as they help the newborn calf stand up and find its mother's udders, gently nudging the mother into the right position.

I've watched this happen with the herd of dairy cows over the fence so many times. I guess it's that direct experience of such a shiny moment that makes the facts of what happens next so hard to watch. Mothers separated from distressed babies. Male calves destined for the 'veal truck'. I know you know all the arguments. I do too. That's why we have rescued three lovely steers across the years. But how many of us get that experience first hand? To arrive at the point where we base decisions on a genuine kinship with another animal is a seriously powerful thing. There's no punishment or judgement, on our behalf or the other animal's. It's just kindly recognising the desire in each other to lead a good life. Reconnection with nature, in the way moving to this hill has given, has taught us so much. There's always more to learn. And more to care about.

Although some of my very early recipes used dairy, we never have it in our fridge anymore. That was a gradual thing, though. More knowledge leads to different thoughts and actions, and that's what led to this butter — because let's be honest, no one wants olive oil under their jam on toast. And don't worry about the turmeric. The flavour isn't really noticeable — it's included more for that beautiful golden buttery colour.

Place all the ingredients in a high-speed blender and blitz until smooth. The colder they are before you start, the better your butter will be. You don't want the mixture to get any hotter than about 20°C (70°F). Starting with cold ingredients will allow the butter to be whipped and aerated longer in the blender, so it'll be softer and more luscious when you spread it.

Jar immediately and refrigerate. The butter will keep in an airtight jar in the fridge for up to 6 months.

Macadamia Parmesan

Makes about 180 g (6 oz)

GLUTEN FREE

160 g (5½ oz) raw
macadamia nuts

15 g (½ oz) nutritional
yeast flakes

10 g (2¼ teaspoons) salt

Even though this barely classifies as a recipe because it is so simple, I wanted
to share it so you can have it on hand to add that familiar cheesy intensity
we all associate with parmesan sprinkled across pasta, salads and soup. I make
this in small batches because macadamia nuts are so high in oil that it can lose
its salty tang if stored for too long

Keeping any leftovers in a tightly sealed jar in the fridge really helps keep it
tasting as though you've just made it, but I wouldn't expect it to last beyond a
month. My husband and I have no problem eating it before then, so I'm sure
you won't struggle to get through it once you've tasted it.

You'll find it on my Cauliflower Soup (page 129), but you could easily add
this to almost any soup. It's a given with homemade pesto, or any pasta really.
And if you love avocado on toast, sprinkling it with this macadamia parmesan
could be a game changer.

Simply blitz all the ingredients in a food processor until they pull together
and resemble crumbs. Store in the fridge in tightly sealed jars and use within
1 month.

Wholefood Vegie Stock Paste

Makes just over 1 kg (2 lb 4 oz) of paste

GLUTEN FREE

250 g (9 oz) leeks

200 g (7 oz) fennel

200 g (7 oz) carrots

250 g (9 oz) celery

100 g (3½ oz) parsley, roughly chopped

100 g (3½ oz) coriander (cilantro), roughly chopped

60 g (2 oz) sun-dried tomatoes in oil

10 g (⅓ oz) garlic cloves (about 2 cloves), peeled

35 g (1¼ oz) salt

I would be lost in the kitchen without this wholefood stock paste. Definitely make this before you start cooking from this book, because it features heavily in many of my recipes. I know you'll quickly find it indispensable whenever you're after the concentrated punch of flavour often found in a stock cube. With this method there's no reduction-boiling for hours — and you get all the fibre from the garden-fresh vegetables and herbs rather than it going into the compost.

Because it is preserved with salt, it has a full spectrum of foundational flavour, whether you use it in a similar way to a 'sofrito' and fry it in some olive oil in a pan before adding vegies for soup or pasta, or rice for risotto, or simply add a generous teaspoon to boiling water for an instant broth or ready-to-go liquid stock.

Feel free to mix up the herbs or vegies based on your personal preference, but don't be tempted to pull back on the salt, because its preservative action will allow this stock paste to keep in the fridge for many months. And you probably won't need to add further salt to your cooking — it's an all-in-one.

You can always use a powdered stock as a substitute in my recipes; you'll just need to adjust for salt and liquid.

Wash the leeks really well, then trim and cut into rounds. Thoroughly wash the fennel and carrots, leaving the skin on the carrots, and cut into 2–3 cm (¾–1¼ in) chunks, along with the celery.

Place all the ingredients, except the salt, in a food processor.

Blitz until the mixture has the consistency of a fresh curry paste; it won't be perfectly smooth, because you don't want soup. Leave a bit of texture in there, but just make sure there are no obvious large bits of any ingredients. Add the salt and blitz again just to mix through.

Immediately seal in jars and store in the fridge, where it will keep for about 6 months. So much goodness in each spoonful!

Green Miso Paste

*Makes about 650 g
(1 lb 7 oz) of paste*

200 g (7 oz) white soy
bean miso paste

200 ml (7 fl oz) extra
virgin olive oil

25 g (1 oz) fresh ginger,
peeled

20 g (¾ oz) coriander
(cilantro) leaves
and stems

12 g (½ oz) rosemary
leaves

200 g (7 oz) Wholefood
Vegie Stock Paste
(opposite)

Another favourite go-to of mine for many reasons, this is like a super-charged version of miso paste. You can use it anywhere you would use miso — with boiling water as a healthy version of cup-a-soup, in a noodle bowl, in burgers, massaged into vegies before roasting, as a broth for dumplings, the list goes on... And because it is based on my Wholefood Vegie Stock Paste (page 232), you can also use it as a flavour foundation in the same way you would a stock powder or liquid stock.

Feel free to vary the fresh herbs, remembering that this is a concentrate, so don't be afraid to use stronger flavours together. I always opt for a white soy bean miso as the base so the colour remains really fresh once the green herbs are added, but if you prefer the flavour of a darker red miso, use that instead.

You won't need to add any further salt to this paste because there is already quite a lot in the stock, and miso is salty on its own anyway. It's worth making a decent batch to have on hand in the fridge, as you'll likely whip through it, especially during soup weather, and whenever you have a hankering for Spelt Dumplings with Nettle & Green Miso Broth (page 148) or Whole Miso-Roasted Cauliflower (page 160).

Place all the ingredients, except the vegie stock paste, in a food processor and blitz until smooth. Once you have an evenly textured paste, add the vegie stock and blitz again to mix through.

Immediately seal in jars and store in the fridge, where the paste will keep for about 6 months.

Green Gomasio

Makes about 1 kg
(2 lb 4 oz)

GLUTEN FREE

150 g (5½ oz) sunflower
seeds

150 g (5½ oz) pepitas
(pumpkin seeds)

150 g (5½ oz) black
sesame seeds

150 g (5½ oz) white
sesame seeds

200 g (7 oz) salt

100 g (3½ oz) chia seeds

3 nori sheets, torn
into 3–4 cm (1¼–1½ in)
pieces

3 g (1 tablespoon) dried
orange zest

I fell in love with gomasio when I first went to Japan. Although traditionally it is made from just sesame seeds and salt, when I decided to make it at home I wanted to add as many different seeds as possible. I added nori because I don't eat enough of it, and even small amounts of nori help add most essential vitamins and minerals to your diet, as well as that unmistakable umami flavour. Orange zest went in too, because that pop of citrus against the saltiness takes this gomasio into completely new territory. Delicious territory.

There's little that doesn't improve with the 'gomasio treatment'. Sprinkle it on salads, over noodle bowls and soups, on sushi, popcorn, avocado on toast, and vegies before you roast them.

Even more amazingly, this simple unsung hero adds seven extra plants to your diet just by being sprinkled across a meal. And if we should be aiming for 30 different plants a day to really keep our microbiome and gut health humming along, then we're already a good way there before lunch if gomasio joins Kale on Toast (page 27) for breakfast.

This recipe makes a big batch — but any smaller and my food processor struggles to chop the seeds as there's not enough bulk to process. You won't have a problem getting through this amount within a few months, though, and it also makes a lovely gift if you'd like to share.

Preheat your oven to 180°C (350°F).

Mix together the sunflower seeds, pepitas and all the sesame seeds and spread out evenly on a baking tray. Bake for 5–7 minutes, or until the white sesame seeds start to colour, and you can smell the toasted aroma of the other seeds.

Remove from the oven and cool, then place the toasted seeds in a food processor with the salt, chia seeds, nori and orange zest. Blitz until roughly chopped and evenly mixed through. The final consistency should resemble breadcrumbs, rather than peanut butter.

The gomasio will keep in an airtight jar at room temperature, out of direct sunlight, for up to 3 months.

Poached Quinces

Serves 2–4

GLUTEN FREE

quinces

water

sugar

vanilla bean, split in
half lengthways

OPTIONAL SPICES

cinnamon stick

cardamom pods

cloves

star anise

Quinces have a relatively short season in autumn, but that doesn't mean you can't have quinces ready to pull out of the freezer for cakes (page 190), to add to a bowl of granola (page 67) or layer across a piece of puff pastry for a quick galette to finish a meal.

We planted a quince tree as soon as we organised running water for our place, and now that tree is giving us fruit each season. The trick is how to stretch the quince season, because nothing is really comparable to quince.

I slice quinces with a mandoline and dry the pieces in my dehydrator to add to our tea blends. Aside from that, poaching has been my favourite method to keep the good quince times rolling throughout the year. I also love pot-roasting them in Maggie Beer fashion, but that takes a lot longer and I can't fit as many in a saucepan. If you have a quince tree, or come across quinces at a farmers' market, here's a reliable way to cook them to use in as many different recipes as you can think of.

I've given ratios, rather than exact amounts, so you can make this recipe work for the quantity of quinces you would like to poach.

Use your hands, or a vegetable brush, to rub the 'fuzz' off the quince skins under running water, but don't peel them.

Cut the quinces into quarters and remove the core and seeds. Place the quince pieces in a large, deep saucepan and cover with water, counting the cups of water as you add them to the pot. For every cup of water you add, stir in 25 g (1 oz) sugar (about 2 tablespoons). Add the vanilla bean and your choice of whole spices and bring to the boil.

Once the sugar has dissolved in the boiling liquid, reduce the heat and simmer for about 1 hour, or until the quince is tender enough that a fork easily penetrates the fruit.

Leave the quince to cool in the poaching liquid. Either remove the fruit with a slotted spoon and freeze for later use, or store in the poaching liquid in the fridge for up to a week.

I tend to put the poached fruit straight into the freezer and keep the poaching liquid in a separate jar in the fridge, so I can reduce the liquid further in a saucepan to make a quince jelly or to use as a glaze for tarts and buns.

Homemade Tofu

*Makes a 400 g (14 oz)
block of firm tofu, if using
a tofu press*

GLUTEN FREE

300 g (10½ oz) dried
soy beans, soaked
overnight in plenty of
cold water

1.65 litres (56 fl oz) water

15 g (½ oz) nigari
(available in Japanese
specialty stores)

For me, tofu sits in the same realm of cooking as bread. Yes, you can easily buy both at the shops, but how utterly satisfying is it to make your own? Making tofu at home is not difficult at all, but there *are* a few steps, and they need to be adhered to, in much the same way that bread-making dictates.

I find the process similar to making a fresh curds-and-whey cheese: first you make soy milk, and then a coagulant is added to split the solids from the liquid. Nigari (magnesium chloride) is the coagulant used in tofu, which you can source online or from a Japanese food specialist store. I buy organic whole dried soy beans in bulk because we make tofu every week, but even if you buy a smaller amount from the supermarket, you'll be surprised at how economical homemade tofu is compared to anything packaged.

I first started making tofu after receiving the best birthday present ever from my husband, in the form of a traditional wooden press made from hinoki (Japanese cypress). If you don't want to invest in a tofu press just yet, you can try straining the tofu more like a fresh cheese, using muslin (cheesecloth) and a metal strainer over a bowl. This will result in more of a silken tofu because it won't be pressed — but silken tofu is also a glorious thing.

You will need to start this recipe the night before, by soaking the soy beans.

Soak the dried soy beans overnight in plenty of water.

Next day, transfer the soy beans to the jug of a high-speed blender, with as much of the soaking water as the jug can hold. Blitz until smooth.

Tip the smooth soy bean mixture into a large saucepan. Pour in the fresh water and bring to the boil, stirring and watching so the mixture doesn't quickly overrun the saucepan — which can happen very easily if not observed!

Once it comes to the boil, remove from the heat. Line a sieve with muslin (cheesecloth) and set it over another large saucepan. Strain the liquid through; this is the soy milk that will become the tofu. You can dispose of the soy bean pulp in your compost.

Bring the milk in the saucepan to the boil, then simmer for 8 minutes over medium heat. This mixture won't boil over as quickly as before, but you'll still need to watch and stir to make sure it doesn't stick to the bottom of the pan.

After simmering for 8 minutes, turn the heat off and add the nigari, barely stirring it through the soy milk. The more you stir at this stage, the larger the curds will be; I love smooth tofu, so I only do a single stir-through to incorporate the nigari. You'll see the curds start to separate. Leave this mixture in the saucepan for 15 minutes to fully separate the tofu curd.

Set up your tofu press, lined with muslin (cheesecloth), over a wire rack in the sink. Pour the curd mixture into the tofu press, allowing the excess liquid to slowly drain through the cloth and down the sink, leaving the curds in the tofu press.

Once most of the liquid has drained through, wrap the cloth over the tofu curds and cover with the wooden press. Apply a weight, such as a can of beans or a litre of soy milk, on top of the wooden press, to further extract the liquid from the curd.

I leave the weighted tofu press overnight in the fridge, on a plate to catch any further liquid. In the morning you can gently remove the tofu from the press and unwrap. So satisfying!

If you would like to keep the tofu in the fridge, store the block in an airtight container. I pour about 60 ml (¼ cup) water over the tofu, to make sure it doesn't dry out. It will then keep for up to a week in the fridge.

Seasonal Masalas &
Homemade Mixed Spice

Freshly ground spice is everything to a curry, or cake — and in the same way that any highly aromatic food can lose its potency over time, spices can definitely wane in the brightness of their flavour once ground. I will often pull out a packet of pre-ground spice if time's against me, but if I'm wanting to really enjoy the process of cooking, and access that space that dissolves time, when all senses are fully immersed in the smells and sounds of making something, then dry-roasting a bespoke mix of spices in a pan and grinding them with a mortar and pestle is absolutely part of the deal.

If you've ever considered Ayurveda the kind of thing that waits to be learned about in your far-off future, you're not alone. I've always loved the idea of Ayurvedic medicine, but never knew how to actually apply it in my everyday life without running off to study it for years, as my gorgeous friend and yoga teacher, Jess, did. As soon as she told me about the benefits of eating certain spices at certain times of the year, I had my edible 'in' to Ayurvedic teachings.

I love everything about letting intuition get involved in choosing spices and seeds, so don't be afraid to wing it based on feel once you get the hang of using your sense of smell to tell you what your body needs — especially when wandering around your garden, literally picking whatever is seasonally abundant and takes your fancy at the time. It's another reason to let your garden go through every growing cycle, giving you a 'living' spice aisle in your vegie patch, yielding things like fennel seeds, coriander seeds, herbs and chillies. It's meditation that comes with a meal.

Each of the following four masalas will give you enough to base a curry around — or, with the homemade mixed spice, to bake a cake with. As much as possible, try to make them just before using, rather than making a big batch and storing it.

Use masalas generously over roasted vegetables, as well as in dal, kitchari (page 156) and with any grains or pulses. These masalas are also delicious to dip sourdough bread into with olive oil, so don't just keep them for Indian-style dishes, use them everywhere!

HOMEMADE MIXED SPICE

10 g (⅓ oz) cinnamon bark

5 g (⅛ oz) coriander seeds

5 g (⅛ oz) whole mace

3 g (⅒ oz) grated nutmeg

2 g (1/16 oz) whole cloves

Place all the ingredients in a spice grinder and blitz until smooth. Use in baking, storing any remainder in an airtight jar in a cool cupboard away from direct sunlight.

SPRING MASALA

10 g (1/3 oz) coriander seeds

8 g (1/4 oz) cumin seeds

4 g (1/9 oz) cardamom pods

3 g (1/10 oz) yellow mustard seeds

1 g (1/32 oz) black peppercorns

Dry-roast all the spices in a frying pan over high heat for a minute or two, until they start to pop and release their aromatics. Immediately remove from the heat, tip into a mortar and grind with a pestle until powdered. Remove the cardamom husks once the seeds have been released.

SUMMER MASALA

10 g (1/3 oz) coriander seeds

5 g (1/8 oz) poppy seeds

4 g (1/9 oz) cardamom pods

5 g (1/8 oz) fennel seeds

10 saffron threads

Dry-roast the coriander seeds, poppy seeds and cardamom pods in a frying pan over high heat for a minute or two, until they start to pop and release their aromatics. Immediately remove from the heat and tip into a mortar. Add the fennel seeds and saffron and grind with a pestle until powdered.

AUTUMN MASALA

20 g (3/4 oz) white sesame seeds

6 g (1/5 oz) celery seeds

3 g (1/10 oz) brown mustard seeds

3 g (1/10 oz) black peppercorns

Dry-roast all the spices in a frying pan over high heat for a minute or two, until they start to pop and release their aromatics. Immediately remove from the heat, tip into a mortar and grind with a pestle until powdered.

WINTER MASALA

8 g (1/4 oz) cumin seeds

5 g (1/8 oz) caraway seeds

3 g (1/10 oz) yellow mustard seeds

2–4 dried red chillies

3 g (1/10 oz) ground turmeric

Dry-roast the cumin seeds, caraway seeds, mustard seeds and chillies in a frying pan over high heat for a minute or two, until they start to pop and release their aromatics. Immediately remove from the heat and tip into a mortar. Add the turmeric and grind with a pestle until powdered.

Red Lentil Sprouts

GLUTEN FREE

70 g (2½ oz) dried
organic baby red lentils

Just about any variety of pulse, grain or seed can be sprouted. I have always sprouted baby red lentils as my first choice; feel free to try lots of other options such as chickpeas, broccoli seeds, mung beans or kidney beans, as they'll all add a good hit of protein and vitamin C to your diet.

When sprouting, always start with organic produce, because that way you can be assured it hasn't been irradiated, and will simply need water to activate its life force and grow a little sprout tail.

The other critical thing — as with anything you are trying to germinate — is to keep the pulses, grains or seeds moist, but not sitting in water. I've found the easiest way is to use a sprouting bag, which you can buy from health food stores or online. Mine is made from hemp, with a drawstring at the top. I hang it over my kitchen tap, so the sprouts have the moisture of the fabric bag available without drowning in water.

I love the process of growing sprouts; it's like having a tiny garden on my kitchen sink. I grow sprouts every week because they're best really fresh, and you can leave them in the fridge to add to salads, sandwiches, soups, stir-fries and curries. Once you have sprouts in your life, you won't have any trouble finding ways to eat them.

Soak the lentils in a bowl of cold water overnight.

Next morning, pour the soaked lentils into a clean sprouting bag and, with the top of the bag open, let tap water run through the lentils. Turn off the water, tighten the drawstring and hang the bag from your kitchen tap to drain.

Simply repeat the process of running water through the lentils in the bag each day, then allowing them to drain over the sink, until their little sprout tails appear. This usually takes 3–4 days.

Once the lentils have sprouts, transfer to an airtight container and store in the fridge. Use within 5–7 days.

Sprouted Almonds

GLUTEN FREE

Years ago, I put sprouted almonds in a salad at our restaurant in Bangkok, and although they are the easiest thing in the world to do, everyone asked me how they were made. The thing is, there's no real 'making' to speak of: you simply soak whole almonds in their skins in plenty of water.

It's the textural change in the almonds that I think everyone loved so much in the salad; they end up tasting a bit like water chestnuts. I have them in my fridge all the time. Not only are they delicious in salads, they make a great snack for those who stand with the fridge door open asking 'What can I eat?' — as well as a gorgeous addition to a pre-dinner plate of olives, Dill Cucumbers with Green Tea & Vine Leaves (page 182) and Pickled Fennel Flowers (page 170).

There's no recipe as such — just take as many whole raw almonds as you think you will eat in a week and put them in a jar filled with water. Pop the jar of almonds in the fridge and you can eat them after a couple of hours, when they're all juicy with hydration. The really beautiful detail in their skin is all the more pronounced after soaking.

You could literally add these almonds to every single salad in this book, but they're especially good in the Snow Pea, Tofu, Nashi, Green Tea & Arame Salad (page 89) or scattered over a plate of Preserved Lemon Hummus (page 32).

Kept in water, the almonds will last for at least a week in the fridge. If you'd like to extend that, change the soaking water every couple of days. The temperature of the fridge will stop the almonds fermenting, so as long as they are kept cold, they will be beautifully fresh to bite into.

Bespoke Flour Mix

Makes about 735 g
(1 lb 10 oz)

150 g (5½ oz) dried black
turtle beans

100 g (3½ oz) dried baby
red lentils

150 g (5½ oz) rolled oats

150 g (5½ oz) sunflower
seeds

150 g (5½ oz) sesame
seeds

30 g (1 oz) whole-leaf
kukicha tea (or your
favourite loose-leaf tea)

5 g (⅛ oz) dried rose
petals

Making your own flour blends takes your involvement in cooking to a whole new level, and I'd also argue it lets your intuition take a front seat, allowing you to pick and choose exactly what takes your fancy in the moment rather than thinking of flour as a single (white, wheat-based) option.

I love wheat flour, but there are so many other kinds to bake with that the idea of blending your own flours can feel like discovering a whole new frontier of food. Go wild. Literally. Add seeds and flowers and whole tea leaves, and all of a sudden baking bread is your own bespoke creation, unlike any other. When I started blending my own flour, it reignited my interest in baking and I looked at everything as a potential addition to my next mix — could I blend whole black beans into flour? How about dried rose petals from our garden, or citrus zest? Yes, is the answer.

A couple of things will make this process possible. The first is a high-speed blender with blades that can handle whole dried pulses and grains. I use my Vitamix and blend in small amounts so as not to overheat the machine; you could also use a spice blender. The second thing that really helps is having a regular baking cycle, so that the flour you mill and blend is always super fresh, because that's the major point of difference to using store-bought, ready-milled flour. Having said that, I don't want to put you off blending your own flour if you don't have a way to mill whole grains, so as an alternative, you can always buy ready-milled flours and mix them together, as I've suggested for the gluten-free blend opposite. You'll still be able to enjoy the creative process of using so many other flours besides just wheat.

The other thing I will say is that because most of the ingredients you'll likely use in your own blends might be gluten free by nature, only ever use your bespoke flour blend as a small percentage — no more than 10% — of your overall mix. So, if you are making a sourdough loaf that usually calls for a total 1000 g (1 kg/1 lb 2 oz) of wheat or spelt flour, then you can substitute 100 g (3½ oz) of that with your bespoke blend, leaving the remaining 900 g (2 lb) as wheat or spelt. If you push it too much past 10%, you might run into trouble with gluten activation and hydration variances. The same applies to making buns, cakes, pasta dough or gnocchi.

Blitz the black turtle beans on their own, so you don't overheat your high-speed blender. Once you have a fine flour, pour into a bowl and continue working through the remaining ingredients in the same way, milling the grains and seeds into flour, one by one, and tipping them into the bowl.

Once you have blitzed all the ingredients to a fine flour, mix thoroughly in the bowl and allow to cool if you have any residual heat in the flour.

Store in an airtight jar in a cool place away from direct sunlight. This flour mix will keep for months, but is so much more special if used within 4 weeks, before it starts to lose its aroma. The smell of freshly milled flour is incredible.

Gluten-Free Flour Blend

*Makes about 1 kg
(2 lb 4 oz)*

GLUTEN FREE

150 g (5½ oz) quinoa
flour

150 g (5½ oz) amaranth
flour

150 g (5½ oz) millet flour

150 g (5½ oz) brown
rice flour

100 g (3½ oz) white
rice flour

100 g (3½ oz) buckwheat
flour

100 g (3½ oz) tapioca
flour

100 g (3½ oz) potato
starch

I only ever use this gluten-free blend in cakes — not in bread baking. I know there are successful gluten-free sourdough bakers out there, but I'm not one of them. If you would like to make any of the cakes in this book gluten free, you can substitute the following blend in a 1:1 ratio for the spelt or rye flour in the original recipe. You may notice the cake is a little denser, but because cake doesn't rely on gluten activation for its success, you'll still have a delicious result.

This mix is based on a proven protein-to-starch ratio, so it's best to stick exactly to this recipe to make sure you can substitute it at a 1:1 ratio for any cakes in this book.

Simply weigh out all the individual flours and mix thoroughly. I mix my flour in a clean bucket with a lid, then store it somewhere nice and cool. Even better if you can fit the flour in your freezer, where it will last so much longer without the risk of bugs appearing, which often come with the organic flours I use. Check all the different flours to see the shortest expiry date on the packaging, and use the blend before that date.

Oatcakes

Makes about 18

225 g (8 oz) rolled oats

110 g (3¾ oz) spelt flour, plus extra for dusting

85 g (3 oz) Turmeric Butter (page 230)

3 g (½ teaspoon) salt

4 g (⅛ oz) baking powder

cold water, to bind the dough

You won't find a lot of biscuit recipes in this book, because in all honesty if I make biscuits, I eat biscuits, and I really don't need to eat biscuits all the time! How does that saying go? Rely on forward planning, not willpower. Something like that.

If I have friends coming for afternoon tea, or it's a long weekend and I feel like having something special, then I'll make these oatcakes. Because they're just sweet enough but also have a savoury bite of salted butter, they work just as well with a cup of tea as they do with almond ricotta; one of those rare things in life.

I first had oatcakes when we were living in London years ago — and then, when we were able to have them in their land of origin, we ate them the whole way around Scotland. So many good memories come with oatcakes for me, but I particularly love the way a simple stamp with the base of a cut-glass sugar bowl makes these so pretty in a farmhouse kind of way.

If you don't have a batch of Turmeric Butter in the fridge, use a good dairy-free butter.

Preheat your oven to 190ºC (375ºF). Line a baking tray with baking paper.

In a food processor, blitz the rolled oats until you have a fine flour. Add the spelt flour and butter and process until the mixture resembles fine breadcrumbs. Add the salt, baking powder and just enough cold water to bind the dough — adding the water in small amounts so you don't end up with a dough that is too sticky.

Turn the dough out onto a floured surface and roll out to approximately 5 mm (¼ in) thick. Cut into discs using a cookie cutter or the rim of a drinking glass. If you have a milk jug or sugar bowl with a cut-glass pattern in the base, dip this in flour and use it to press a stamped pattern onto your oatcakes.

Place the oatcakes on the baking tray and bake for 15–20 minutes, until firm. Cool on a wire rack before adding to a cheese board or enjoying with a cup of tea. These will keep in an airtight container for at least a week.

Chocolate-Dipped Fennel Flowers

freshly cut unsprayed
fennel flower heads

dark chocolate
(dairy-free)

I really want you to try these little flavour bombs. Even if you don't have fennel in your garden, a drive down a dirt road in the country will likely give you a chance to forage for fennel flowers if you're up for an adventure with your chocolate fix!

I first made these when we were filming the TV series and we needed something to tick the dessert box, but I didn't happen to have the iconic 'one I'd prepared earlier'. I always have dark chocolate, and I also had fennel flowers — so if you like those choc-coated licorice bullet lollies, you might have a small conniption over these. Mine was quite public.

And for all the times you haven't made dessert, or a little something sweet, 10 minutes is all that stands between you and these special delights. Pick them up by the stem, pop them in your mouth and bite off the flower. The best.

Snip the fennel flower heads into individual flower stems, leaving the stem intact as a 'handle' for dipping and picking up to eat.

Melt the dark chocolate in a double boiler, or a heatproof bowl set over a saucepan of simmering water.

Individually dip each fennel flower into the melted chocolate to just cover the flower. Place on a sheet of baking paper and leave to set in the fridge for about 15 minutes. These can be prepared up to a day ahead of eating.

Discard the stem once you've bitten off the chocolate-coated flower.

an extra-large thank you

I'm sitting here wondering if being able to properly convey my thanks isn't the most difficult part of this book's process, considering I've started this page four times over! There are a couple of reasons for my stumbling in this regard, the first being that I'm thankful to every single person I've ever cooked for, or eaten with, because they have all played a part in this book being something I can hold in my hands and not just in my mind. Kind of impossible to make a list from that, though. And secondly, how on earth do I make sure my thanks carry all the weight of the gratitude that comes from so many unique experiences? The last thing I want is for this to come across as a casual thanks-for-that. It's anything but thanks-lite. This is a full-fat thank you. For all the time, and energy, and care and cups of tea from so many. So in that spirit, my very generous and very warmest thanks go to...

The amazing team at Murdoch Books, including Justin Wolfers, Sarah Odgers, Katri Hilden, Vanessa Masci and of course Jane Willson, who set these fantastic wheels in motion over lunch in Melbourne that day in May. I feel like I waited at least eight years from the moment I had the thought of wanting to do a book until I had the chance to make that happen. But after meeting you all, I'm pretty sure I was just waiting for the best publication team that ever there was. I wasn't kidding when I said I would miss seeing your emails in my inbox on a weekly basis. I have absolutely loved being guided through this process by you all and your unfaltering grace.

To Henrie Stride, for being in my corner throughout those never-ending auditions that landed me my first job on Channel 9 in Sydney all those years ago, and ever since. Thank you for each and every time you've gone in to bat for me, I couldn't have hoped for a better champion in this life. You're such a rare and good sort Henrie.

To Lean Timms, Lee Blaylock and Gill Radford for six days of non-stop food-focused effort, fuelled by tea and opera in the morning and cake and 80s tunes in the afternoon — you are magicians, my friends, and the memory of shooting my first cookbook with you all will forever be on my favourites list. It was so amazing to live each of the photos in this book, rather than just set them up to shoot. Thank you for caring so much. I hope everyone who cooks from this book can feel how much we all loved creating it together.

To Maggie Beer, not only for your beautiful foreword, but also for every inspiration you offered me over so many years of working together. I feel like I packed so many moments into my pockets for later being around you, and then drew on every single one of them when it came time to create this book. You have such a crazy and amazing life, I'm not sure how there was any room for our paths to cross, but I'm very glad they did.

To Amy Chaplin, another incredible source of inspiration. I absolutely love your whole approach to food (and tea obsession to rival my own), and will be forever grateful for your casual query as to when I'd be doing a cookbook all those years ago. It made me laugh at the time because I couldn't imagine ever being in such a position, but you planted a seed, and not for the first time, I felt such a kinship with you despite the physical distance between us.

To Tony Lewis — you take a mighty fine photo, my friend! Thank you so much for driving to the Barossa time and again across the year, to jump in my collie-infused ute and go on a mad, cross-country dash, chasing golden light across the hills. After so many years working together, it's such a joy to see our farm and familiar backroads through your magical lens.

To my family and friends, for eating all the weird with the wonderful along the way.

And finally to DT, for growing most of the food we eat and bringing it into the kitchen as though it was the most precious gift anyone could ever receive, because we both know it is.

Index

Published in 2024 by Murdoch Books, an imprint of Allen & Unwin

Murdoch Books Australia
Cammeraygal Country
83 Alexander Street
Crows Nest NSW 2065
Phone: +61 (0)2 8425 0100
murdochbooks.com.au
info@murdochbooks.com.au

Murdoch Books UK
Ormond House
26–27 Boswell Street
London WC1N 3JZ
Phone: +44 (0) 20 8785 5995
murdochbooks.co.uk
info@murdochbooks.co.uk

For corporate orders and custom publishing, contact our business development team at salesenquiries@murdochbooks.com.au

Publisher: Jane Willson
Editorial manager: Justin Wolfers
Design manager: Sarah Odgers
Designer: Vanessa Masci
Editor: Katri Hilden
Photographer: Lean Timms
Additional photography: Tony Lewis
Stylist: Lee Blaylock
Assistant chef on shoot: Gill Radford
Production director: Lou Playfair

Text © Cherie Hausler 2024
The moral right of the author has been asserted.
Design © Murdoch Books 2024
Photography © Lean Timms 2024, except pages 4, 7, 10, 11, 13, 24, 52, 71 (top), 86, 101, 108, 136, 144 (top), 166, 176 (bottom), 184, 204, 214 (top), 224, 256 © Tony Lewis 2024
Cover photography © Lean Timms 2024

Murdoch Books acknowledges the Traditional Owners of the Country on which we live and work. We pay our respects to all Aboriginal and Torres Strait Islander Elders, past and present.

ISBN 9 781 92261 674 6

A catalogue record for this book is available from the National Library of Australia

A catalogue record for this book is available from the British Library

Colour reproduction by Splitting Image Colour Studio Pty Ltd, Wantirna, Victoria
Printed by 1010 Printing International Limited, China

The information provided within this book is for general inspiration and informational purposes only. While we try to keep the information up-to-date and correct, the author and publisher do not assume and hereby disclaim any liability to any party for any loss, damage, or disruption caused by errors or omissions, whether such errors or omissions result from negligence, accident, or any other cause. Be sure to check with your local council and use common sense when handling any potentially harmful equipment or materials.

OVEN GUIDE: You may find cooking times vary depending on the oven you are using. All oven temperatures listed are fan-forced unless otherwise stated. If you require the conventional oven temperature, increase the given temperature by 15–20°C (25–35°F), according to the manufacturer's instructions.

TABLESPOON MEASURES: We have used 20 ml (4 teaspoon) tablespoon measures. If you are using a 15 ml (3 teaspoon) tablespoon add an extra teaspoon of the ingredient for each tablespoon specified.

10 9 8 7 6 5 4 3 2 1

MIX
Paper | Supporting
responsible forestry
FSC® C016973